The Wave

(Touching Memoirs from life)

By different writers

Edited By: Salwa Elhamamsy

Dedication

To my lovely family,

To my mother's soul,

To you, dear reader.

Thanks

To Aisling Meath for proofreading.

5

Introduction

How many waves do we face in life that might hit us? shake us, deluge us, but they wash over us. In the end, nothing remains except a taste of saltiness that stays in our throats. It disappears, however, with a sip of water.

Do you know the moment when you reach the tip of your happiness? When the smile fills your face? When you receive congratulations on your success, the moment of success that you have been eager to realize, that you have been looking forward to with all your heart? Do you know what it is when someone feels the opposite of all that? When the moment of happiness turns into deep sadness, turns into sorrow? You find yourself looking for yourself, wishing to find any ray of light to guide you.

Who among us has not suffered in this life at some point? Who has not found dark, narrow paths in life to get through before adjusting his sails and setting a new course? It might even be happening right now.

In March 2015, I was celebrating a beautiful achievement. Two of my books, a collection of short stories and a memoir of my travels in Ireland, were being launched at the Irish Writers Centre in Dublin. As an Arab writer having lived for four years in Ireland, it meant a lot to me to have my works translated into English. The event was a success, and everyone congratulated me.

I did not expect the bad news I got the following day when the doctor informed me that I had cancer.

Yes, the word that one may even avoid spelling out.

This news plunged me from the top of the clouds into a deep sea of anxiety, pushing me down a strange path that I never expected to walk.

After the first visit to the doctor, I decided to write about this experience. I prayed to God that this would be only a single chapter in my life and in my book, a chapter that would go quickly and without pain.

In this heart-warming book, I collected many stories by many authors from different countries. Each wrote about a touching personal life experience. In describing the challenges that each of us struggled with and finally overcame, I hope to inspire optimism in the reader.

We all face the waves of life that threaten to overwhelm us, submerge us and carry us on a current we don't expect. These stories show that we can flow with those currents and be renewed just as the tide washes up to the shore.

Are you ready then to set sail in our memoirs? Please do, and do not worry about The Wave, It will pass.

The Editor.

Chapter 1

The Wave

Salwa Elhamamsy

Translated by: Kareem Mostafa

This is my face. These are my eyelashes. I see my eyebrows too. I look at the woman in the mirror. I finally get reunited with my features again

They're back at last. Or is it I that returned to them? Thank God for everything after all.

I resemble winter as much as it resembles me. I watch a bird flying in the distance. Sitting lonely on a tree branch. A branch devoid of leaves. I finally see the entire tree, which is completely leafless.

I observe his fluffy feathers, his tiny head tucked cosily between his delicate wings.

His eyes sleepy from a day's worth of flight on this frosty winter morning. How can he be so sleepy when we're just starting a new day? Or might he just be upset because of his loneliness? He might be waiting for a friend perhaps, or several friends.

I resemble fall. I enjoy watching how it sketches out the city like a portrait with golden and crimson crusty leaves in the parks and in the streets. My leaves seem as though they have blended with the leaves of Fall. Falling together, filling the spaces around us. Months have passed, and I contemplate the long slender branches of the trees that once bore leaves but don't anymore. Praises be to Him, who brings life back to the world after deadening it in this cycle.

I resemble that bird from earlier. We both keenly await the Spring. The leaves of Spring, the flowers, and the rich, thick trees that are overflowing with colourful, high-spirited birds racing to decorate their new nests. I definitely love Spring.

***

I don't know where to start my story. I do not wish for it to go on for too long, nor for it to be over before you know it.

Standing on the sandy shore, I watched the sea with immense admiration and amazement. In the distance, a beautiful wave was forming. Mixed tones of sapphire blue, cream and white began emerging, racing with its friends to see which will grow first and arrive happily at the shore. Time and time again. This is a typical sight at the beautiful Mediterranean Sea on the north coast of Egypt.

This time it was different. This time this one particular wave was a betrayal. This time, the seemingly innocent wave in the distance began growing and growing. Growing so much in fact, that it was taller than me. So tall - it was futile for me to run back to the shore for safety, there was no point. The wave was going to consume me however I looked at it. I was not alone, my husband, and my two sons were right there next to me, and this wave was about to consume us all. The wave finally came crashing down, submerging all four of us completely as we stood there. We felt that we were going to drown. A few seconds passed, and this wave was now behind us, pulling back quickly beneath our feet back into the sea peacefully to where it came from answering the call of its originator. The shine of the golden sun was back, and the refreshing, adventurous breeze of the sea was upon us again. Everything was fine again, and we had survived.

I woke up from my dream. It was March 2014. I prayed to God to let this be good news for us all. That day I had a doctor's appointment for him to inspect an urgent matter for me.

I was shocked by his words. The doctor took a small skin sample next to where the tumor area was. As he worked the ultrasound machine, I asked him if he saw anything that didn't look all right. He shook his head. He saw some cells that appeared to be cancerous, but he was not sure. He concluded that we would have a confirmed result after a further microscopic inspection procedure was conducted.

Just like that? He shocked me with his directness. Not even an introduction to prepare for me such news.

Blood rushed to my face as I was helped up by the nurse who helped me with my clothes back on. I left the clinic room feeling light-headed at best, with my heart beating relentlessly. I was told I had to wait a whole week to know the final results.

I prayed to Him and hoped for the best. I prayed that it was a false alarm and that everything would be all right. Since he said he wasn't 100% sure it meant there was still hope.

I called two Irish friends of mine, and invited them for lunch in a nearby hotel. I arrived early, and tried to get started on writing the article I was meant to send to an Egyptian newspaper. I was a few days late in sending it. I was barely writing 2-3 lines a day. I wasn't able to think of anything else but the tumor issue.

We sat and engaged in small talk. I was happy to talk about absolutely anything except the matter that consumed my mind. We sat for a short while in the lounge area before moving on to the lunchroom to order some light lunch. We spoke about my recent book launch in the Book Writers Association in Ireland and how it was very well received from their point of view. We spoke about our children, what's happening on the media, and anything but what was truly on my mind the whole time.

It's almost time for the results of the tests from the ultrasound. I take a deep breath and enter the doctor's office. She confirmed at once that indeed they were cancerous cells; but that the good news was that it was a small tumor than could be quickly and easily removed.

"Do you have plans for next week? "she asked "Just a lunch I was planning with a few friends and a radio interview I was meant to be doing about my latest travel-writing book about Ireland'' I answered.

She insisted that I do not cancel any of my plans and that I continue with them as normal.

"I don't want you stopping any of your plans. The cancerous cells have hit your immune system, and by doing things that you love and enjoy you will effectively be strengthening your immune system, which is what we want."

I heard her all right, but how was I going to think about anything like my writing endeavors or my friends after the news I had just received?

She proceeded to book me in for this simple surgery procedure two weeks from today. During the surgery, a few more samples would be taken, and those would in turn be used to dictate the best post-treatment procedures I will have to go through.

It could either be radiotherapy only, or radiotherapy accompanied with chemotherapy. What was I to do if the answer was chemotherapy? God help me get through this.

God only knows what the future holds. Will this end right here and there? Or will, God forbid, this will escalate into other forms and side effects.

I was shocked and unsettled. I felt unable to read or write, or even get into regular conversation with anyone. I recited a few prayers asking for God to heal me and to heal all illnesses in the world in general. Yes I believe in God, just as I am at peace with his decision to have him choose me to go through this. But nevertheless at times I feel a cold fright inside. I resort to my bed, to hide with my feelings and thoughts - especially the voices in my head - all under my quilt. I close my eyes and try to sleep, as I used to when I was a little girl hiding from my mother after she finds that I got bad grades in a school exam.

I pick up a small booklet that they gave me in the hospital, which was meant to calm me down a little. I started reading about how these cancerous cells grow slowly and then reproduce, conquering both the good and the bad cells; I read about how the body weakens and activity slowly reduces.

Sugars, milk products, and red meats suddenly become taboo foods after I learn that these cells feed on them to grow. Instead, I need to increase my intake of rich vegetables and fruit that do not contain a lot of sugar, which would in turn help to produce enzymes and healthy cells to combat the bad ones.

I didn't know what hit me then. A kind of astonishment combined with fear. I sat in silence for a few minutes staring into nothingness. I knew that I had started a journey on a road so foreign to me with no clear end in sight, and no set number of steps for me to complete either. Would there be any obstructions or side paths ahead? Or would I go back after just a few steps in?

"It's a simple case. Just an intense period for a short amount of time, and it will soon dissolve God willing. May God make it easier on you? "

My friend prayed for me. I prayed she was right.

I have faith in God. How can I have faith but still feel all this fear and worry inside me? Isn't my case much less severe than other cases I have heard have who have been affected by this illness? Thank God for everything after all. I always remind myself to keep God in my heart. After all, he is the healer and the saviour. Might this be a test? Yes. I just hope it's not too difficult on me. How can I teach my kids about faith and patience when I carry all this fear myself? Where is my strength and calmness? Be strong. Our lives should not be shaken because of this issue. I have to continue being the strong mum that they've come to know in the face of danger and adversity. Not a weak one.

They asked me to undergo an MRI scan. The cannula they inserted pained me. After that, the nurse came to reassure me that everything would be all right. She will be inserting a medical liquid in my arm - not my chest - a type of technology that will help to generate an image of movement inside my body so they can monitor activity-taking place.

Why wasn't I getting calmer? There seemed nothing to be afraid of? She lays me on a bed, places headphones on my head, and I then find my bed being pulled into a tube-like X ray machine. Both ends were open but inside was claustrophobic and it was hard to feel natural to say the least. Next thing, they started to play soft background music to my ears and after that I started to hear bell sound hits. Despite the headphones and the music, I was clearly able to hear the nurse informing me that she has initiated the imaging process and that it would take approximately 15 minutes.

God's words were my backbone. I found myself reciting different prayers and comforting verses from the Quran as much as I could until I tired. I would then pause to rest a little bit. I felt time was passing by slower than usual. I felt heat rush through my body after the liquid starting spreading further into my body through the cannula they inserted earlier. It didn't take too long before I found myself reaching for the buzzer button that they provided me in case I wanted to stop at anytime "I can't continue anymore".

Watching over the sea, on Greystones beach in Dublin, I stood contemplating the waves. They appeared calm, void of any movement it seemed - except for two small ones racing. I observe the sea foam as it dissolves as soon as it hits the shore. I find myself remembering my wave from the dream I had that one morning. There were no seagulls in my dream like the one I was now seeing at Greystones where I stood. The bird playfully took on the waves, flying close to them as it happily glided and swayed depending on how the wind came.

I see kids playing and laughing, taking turns to skim stones in the sea to see which one can go the furthest.

On my way back to the car I noticed an elderly lady in the car beside me also gazing at the shore from afar. Sitting in her car she seemed as if she was taking in the sights from the distance, as she was unable to walk to the shore. Beside her, another woman, maybe a sister or a friend was talking to her.

On the day of the surgery, I stood in front of the mirror and stared at myself. The preparation of the surgery was harder than the actual surgery. The surgery is painless due to the anaesthesia given, but it was my worry that made it unbearable. The nurse attempted several times to insert the syringe in my arm to begin the process but my blood was afraid to come out. Tears started when the nurse asked my husband to leave me to rest a little bit. Another Irish nurse came into the room and started speaking to me in Arabic.

"Darling, how are you?"

She used to be based in Saudi for several years. Her memory served her well to pick up a few Arabic sentences that she can use when she needed to.

Next, the surgeon came into the room, and she noticed how worried I was. She ordered an aspirin for me to soothe and calm me down. She noticed the tears I was holding back in my eyes, that I was trying to control so that I do not cry in front of her. I felt suffocated and immensely uneasy.

She told me, with her Iraqi dialect "abshy" which meant cry. For it was better to cry and let it out so that I can relax.

The surgeon instructed the nurse to take me to the theatre room where the surgeries in the hospital are performed. As she was transporting me on my bed to the theatre room, she would caress my hand every once in a while talking to me in her broken Arabic-

"Don't worry dear. Don't worry".

She looked into my eyes and smiled as she said it. Quran verses were always on my mind. Various prayers. Especially one that is used for protection, the same words uttered by Moses when he was about to confront the Pharaoh king for the first time. And like that foul king, this foul illness. I signed a paper they requested me to sign confirming my birthdate and the type of surgery I was about to undergo.

Moments later, and the anaesthesia doctor arrived to numb my body so that they can start the procedure. To my surprise, he greeted me in Arabic. Further - that he was Egyptian. He smiled and asked me which of two methods I would prefer to have the anaesthesia delivered to me. He started, making sure to mention God's name for blessings before he began. The Iraqi surgeon returned again to the room. She noticed still some residues of my nervousness. She knelt down and hugged me and prayed for me to be calm and relaxed, and then they began as I slowly dozed off

"Mum... can you hear us? Salwa?"

I opened my eyes to see my sons and husband around me - smiling to me. I honestly did not feel a thing - just nervousness before the surgery, and I was elated and relieved to realize that it was all finally over, or so I felt.

In the hospital room, I recalled how relaxing the anaesthesia was, for I did not feel anything and had a deep, comfortable sleep
After they woke me up I was absolutely wrecked. Still, I proceeded to perform my sunrise prayer noticing that it was almost daytime outside. I kept falling in and out of sleep, but I managed to get it done in the end.

Inside the room, across from my bed, was a portrait of a beautiful town in the west of Ireland called Kinsale. It featured a seaside, with a wave of medium height crashing against the rocks on the shore. It reminded me again of the dream I had earlier before I visited the doctor and realized the illness that I had.

In the morning I look to my right to see a beautiful bouquet of flowers that the nurse had delivered earlier and informed me that it was from one of my friends. Behind the flowers is a big spacious square window overlooking Dublin city where you could see beautiful white houses lined up in the distance across several valleys. Just as soon as I was realizing this I also started hearing the hustle and bustle of the streets outside as well as the sounds of nurses moving about the ward on our floor.

I wait patiently for the results of the procedure. Hopefully it went it all right. I then received a call from my surgeon who assured me that my procedure was completed successfully with no hiccups. The affected area has been removed from my skin and patched up, and there was no evidence of cancerous cells anywhere else in my body.

However, there was another lump that they had discovered and were still unsure as to whether this was also an affected area or benign and unaffected, and they had to more research to find out if a second surgery might be needed. The next step after that would be to decide whether the treatment would be radiotherapy or God forbid, chemotherapy.

After 2 weeks, I was asked to come back for a second surgery. This time I was less afraid because I had already been through the first one and knew that it was not painful and that it was not worth it to be as worried as I was.

The doctors advised me to relax and take a small trip after I'm fully recovered from the surgery and before I begin chemotherapy. We ended up travelling to Lismore, where I participated in an international book conference and where my travel-writing book about Ireland was being sold. I spent a few good days there meeting with readers and other book writers before I had to head back.

Back at the hospital. In my chair I sat to receive the first session of chemotherapy in calmness while I recited some verses from the Quran for blessing and healing. I did not feel any pain after the simple prick of a needle that my nurse gave me. Through this needle the chemotherapy liquid substance was dispersed into my blood. A plastic, transparent bag suspended above my head mounted on a steel stand next to me is where the liquid is contained and originates. At the start, there was a seemingly metallic taste in my mouth when the substance began entering my body. I felt heat once again in my body as the liquid continued to spread. I continued the session, which lasted for about 5 hours.

The first dosage is the strongest they told me, and it was actually very tiring. For approximately a week afterwards I felt weaker day in and day out. There was one particular day where I felt very frail to the point where I asked my husband to call me an ambulance car to take me to the hospital. Every time I felt feelings such as difficulty breathing, or dizziness, or digestive problems, I would call the hospital immediately only for them to assure me that these are normal side effects that are prone to happening. They didn't feel normal to me.

I finally arrived at the hospital feeling extremely ill. I had immense dizziness, low blood pressure, and difficulty breathing all at once.

Even the nurses were surprised when they saw me. The head doctor came to see me and asked me how I was feeling. The only words I could utter were,

"I'm dying".

I remember being in a semi-coma at the time. I would hear sounds around me from time to time, but I remained sleeping.

After a few hours passed of doctors treating me with further liquids and remedies to help make me feel better, I finally started to improve. I was praying to God from time to time to forgive my sins and to heal me. Earlier, it was upon me the feeling that I was going to die after all. The nurse came and sat close to me to hear and to try to understand my raspy voice to figure out if I needed anything. I was barely able to speak and every word I uttered I felt would be one less breath that I would lose and couldn't get back.

Dr. Westhrop, the head doctor, asked me if I needed anything at this time. I nod.

"I want to go back to my natural state"

I remember the look of seriousness in her eyes when she advised

"Be realistic. Not before another week in the hospital"

"Well, I'm refusing chemo treatment"

"I hear you. Let us talk about this when you are feeling better"

Yes I was accepting of what God has sent upon me of illness and exhaustion, but at the same time it was not easy for me to come to terms with this difficult state of living and constant tiredness.

It was not just exhaustion, but it turned me from youthful to old-aged very quickly. Yes I felt much older and frailer than I really was. I started again reciting various prayers that I remembered asking that I survive this illness and that everything would return to normal soon. I was mentally aware that I could die at any moment. Thankfully I found myself getting ever so slightly better over the next few days. Slow improvement yes, but it was better than nothing. I was not able to answer any phone calls from friends in either in Ireland or Egypt.

After about one week, the doctor discharged me and allowed me to return to my home.

After some discussion, she advised me to return to completing my chemotherapy treatment once more and that she would reduce the dosage by 25%,

"I can agree to your wish of stopping chemotherapy, but I do not want to risk seeing you next year with a new cancer." she told me.

This answer gave me the motivation I needed to return to finishing my chemotherapy treatment.

The time came for my second session.

A dear cousin of mine had come to visit from Egypt around that time, and she accompanied me to the hospital to keep me company for this second session. It went well, the nurse installed the medical liquid in the steel apparatus next to where I was sitting. The liquid then dispersed itself gradually through the cannula in my arm and finally through to my bloodstream. I would recite Quran verses for God to protect me from any harm or side effects this might have and to bless with only the best that it can do for me.

I knew that it was poison. Yes, poison. Entering my body and destroying the bad as well as the good cells, and for that reason the doctor always prescribes a suitable dosage for each patient, like a perfumer who constructs a special scent based on their customer's needs. With that, everyone's medicine construct and intake is slightly different, which in turn affects the side effects that each person experiences.

At times, I found myself reading about hair fall during the chemotherapy treatment. I feared this issue a lot. But it was something that was inevitable especially in my case. And the nurses recommended that I cut my hair gradually so that it is not a big shock when the last of my hair falls. And it was not easy. Before going to the hospital for the first surgery, I fixed myself in the mirror, and prepared nice makeup, and brushed my hair a nice way that would suit my now medium-length hair. I asked my husband to take a photo of me for memory. I wanted to take photos of myself while I am in my best of states. I didn't know how long it would take for me to get back to that look again, if ever.

I started feeling some slight pain in the roots of my hair. My hair started to get drier and frailer with time, and I could literally hear a crunching sound, like crushing autumn leaves, every time I ran my fingers through it. The more I'd run my hand against my hair, the more hairs I would see fall to the ground. But it wasn't as scary as I thought it would be, because it was happening gradually and it didn't all happen at once. Bit by bit, I started mustering up the courage and started to remove the rest of it myself day by day until it was all gone; completely, gone. The only thing left was a very faint layer of hair similar to that of a newborn baby.   I was certainly affected by this incident, but I thanked God in acceptance of what had happened. I know that this is but a small test of patience from Him. I reminded myself that there are many others that face much bigger tests than this and even they manage to get through.

My newly purchased wig was really close and central to me during this time. I would wear it at home whenever I missed feeling my hair, and I began to appreciate the importance of having a head full of hair, especially for women, as it is a matter of beauty for her as it is beauty for men as well. Another benefit I discovered of hair is of course heat and keeping me warm. I really felt that especially when I was going out in winters in Ireland, where the cold reached my scalp despite me wearing a headscarf already.

The second session went successfully. I felt intense fatigue after the first week, but the following sessions were nothing compared to that so I managed them pretty well. Especially around this time several family members started flying in to spend some time with me and make sure I'm doing all right. My uncle came with his family over from England, and I spent really beautiful days with them, which helped relieve lots of the pain I was feeling. I was prepared for the third session and I was a lot more confidant and mentally prepared, for I felt the love and support of the people who matter in my life around me.

I had to sit one chemotherapy session once every three weeks. Not a single session would pass by without a tear dropping from my eye from how tired I was. My husband would keep me patient by reminding me that today is Thursday, and that in two days the pain would cease. This was my mental reminder to myself before every session: that it wouldn't take more than two days before I regain my energy back. During those two days I couldn't do much, but after that I would be able to walk with someone who would help support from my shoulders. By the third week I started feeling much more natural. I was now able to go out on my own and even drive. This would go on well until it's time for my next session where I would find myself fit and able to endure it.

I would find myself often thinking about the meaning of life and death, and how death is closer than we think. I thought about how weak man can be in the face of nature. I also thought about achievements, and whether I've achieved what I wanted in life. I started thinking about what can man do in the last portion of his life, not taking for granted this life that they were handpicked to live.

My final chemotherapy session did not pass calmly. I had a cold that I was fighting days before my session, and I was feeling very frail and borderline unconscious. I went to the hospital after two days asking for help, and one of the nurses proceeded to treat me by injecting defence fluids to my weak body. She looked at my pale face and teary eyes as she tried to hide hers and said,

"It's is your last song. I promise you that"
I contemplated what she said, and she inspired me to pull through for this last session. And she was right, indeed it was my last song, and after a few days the cold was gone, and I started to improve.

It was important for me to go on a short trip to regain my energy and enthusiasm. I decided to travel to visit my uncle in Exeter. I spent a few days there and returned a lot more revitalized and ready to start the much lighter radiotherapy sessions.

I was meant to sit thirty-three sessions over the course of a month and a half. It did not hurt at the start but then they asked me stay put for fifty minutes without moving, and that was really tiring. One of the nurses asked if I would like to listen to music to make the time pass by quicker, or if I had a favourite CD that they can play for me. I thought I might as well use this opportunity to listen to Quran instead. I enjoyed listening to one particular Surah. My befriending of the Qur'anic literature made the journey so much easier for me. I started not to feel the time pass by. Finally, the sessions came to an end, but it had taken its toll on my skin. Marks that resembled sun burn. They also hurt just as much as sunburn would. I had to go through that pain for a few days. I wouldn't be able to sleep from the intensity of the pain sometimes.

One night the pain just receded. I slept that night and had an astonishing dream, which brought me immense serenity. I heard the prophet, peace be upon him, speaking to me saying, "there is no God but God" and as if he was consoling me to be patient on what has affected me, and advising me to stay true to my faith in God and in myself.

I woke up happy and optimistic. And sure enough, I started feeling better with every day that passed. I thanked God that things got better and returned to normal. My hair started to slowly grow again which was a great sign. My hair was really short yes, but it was a start. I was excited to get back to my regular social and creative life.

At this stage I had around six sessions of Herceptin that I had to complete. Herceptin, they told me, is a chemical that preserves good cells in the body and targets only the bad cells. I would not feel anything during those sessions especially because every session was barely an hour. In one of those times, I was sitting in the waiting room waiting for my turn to go in, and I noticed an Irish lady looking at me. So I smiled to greet her, and her eyes looked like she was trying to recognize me like she knew me from somewhere, from taking those chemotherapy sessions earlier .

"You used to take chemotherapy sessions next to where my husband was last year," she said,

"Yes" I answered.

"You look so much better, I saw you last year and you seemed to be in constant fatigue. I remember that day, your husband and son was there with you if I recall correctly"

Her words comforted me. "Thank God I feel more natural now," I thought to myself

"I am happy for you. This means there is hope for my husband to get better " she continued

Her husband, who was sitting next to her smiled. He too was on his way to recovery he told me.

The nurse called on me to go in for my session. As I entered, many nurses were greeting me with warm smiles and looks, probably noticing that my state had improved and I'm looking better. This time I was sitting next to an Irish lady. I found out from her after a short chat that this is her second time doing chemotherapy, and that she is taking care of her much older brother and sister who stay at home. I noticed how pure and modest she was. Her life was affected by this illness but despite that she was sure of her calling,

46

to mind her old siblings who needed her in their lives. Even though her illness was on going, she was accepting of it with an open heart and calmness. I complimented her courage and self-control. She told me

"One of my rules is to focus on the positives in my life no matter what"

As I was leaving and grabbing my bag to go, another patient remarked

"You're leaving early today"

"I'm finishing up my last sessions of Herceptin. How are you keeping"? I answered

He replied, with a sad smile that these treatments are like a poison. Nothing but a poison that's bringing his life down.

I told him not to say that. Allow the medicine to enter your body in peace so that you can be fully recovered. Remember that it is a test from God, and that you will be healed God willing but it just takes a little patience So stay patient and positive," I said finally

With the days passing by, I truly started to feel better over all. I returned to my art classes which I had stopped since the fatigue hit me. I drew an oil painting of a beautiful blue boat on the shore of a sea. I was missing the view of the sea in my country Egypt. As I continued to paint, I accentuated the waves and the sea foam accompanying it in blue, turquoise, and white.

One of my colleagues saw the painting and she exclaimed:

"This is beautiful Salwa, wow".

She mentioned she was also drawing a painting with a boat in it by the seaside. I looked at the painting she was working on and I noticed that the boat was broken.

 "Why didn't you draw a working boat-I like to think of boats as a symbol of hope for the future, new horizons. Don't leave it broken- fix the boat!
She smiled and after contemplating what I said, told me she would. "Thank you" she said at last.

From time to time, I still remember that wave that submerged me in my dream, and I ask, myself- "Could it be that the waves have finally settled and the sea is calm again?"

Chapter 2

BROKENHEARTED: A WIDOW'S LAMENT

Creating new hope each step of the way

Patricia Steele

My wedding day. My baby's first tooth. A happy family reunion.

Good memories left behind only to be remembered fleetingly in days to follow. He left me at Christmas. Without my permission. Without my approval. Despite his suffering, my selfish heart demanded he stay. Seeing him fade away before my eyes at Christmas time far from home was so sad, I have no words. But I cling to the memory of the smiles for the grandchildren, for my birthday celebration, his beloved iPad as he played Solitaire and the last wisps of a life well lived. My husband.

The final week of his life was a mixed blessing. I've been told to always look for the silver linings as life throws us a hardball. Sometimes it works. Sometimes it doesn't. As I think about the days and nights surrounding last Christmas, I force myself to remember him as he was then. Ill. Thin. In chronic pain. Wishing for a silent death that would ease his pain. If I can just concentrate on those last days, hoping for a surcease from his daily struggles, my heart can smile knowing he is at peace. When I allow the memory of a robust man, dancing me across the dance floor or pulling me on my water ski, I am lost.

Facing widowhood is difficult, devastating, lonely, hurtful, frightening and often no words can describe the pain. Over the years, I have watched other women whose lips suddenly trembled and tears fell without warning. I felt their pain but could not understand what it truly meant until it happened to me. The silence that clings to a woman whose husband just took their last breath is so loud the thrumming rings in her ears. The words that cascade through her head as she walks silently out of the hospital, knowing she's left the other half of her heart behind her scream through her mind. When she sees her car, she realizes it is now hers, not ours. The enormity of her loneliness and pain follows her every inch of every mile as she drives away with the feel of her husband's forehead still warm against her lips. Forever. Eternity. Never. Those are the words she whispers, knowing she will never feel his lips against hers or hear them say 'I love you' again.

Now, five months later, a box holding his ashes sits on the floor in the closet. The memorial video is complete. The celebration of life party is planned. The marble gravestone is etched with his name, his year of birth and death and has been embedded in the Steele family plot in Virginia. Closure is ahead; in two weeks, a 2,344 mile-road trip of and our family will say their goodbyes. For the widow, it will be the longest goodbye, maybe never. But then the healing will begin.

Each new sunrise brings new hope, new beginnings and new adventures. The silver lining is coming to the surface. Singlehood is becoming easier as long as the memories of those long-ago days of dancing, water skiing, daily projects, healthy laughter and the joy in sharing family get togethers can remain just minutely below the surface. For those are the memories that clog my widow's throat, tighten my chest and bring unsuspecting tears. Those are the memories that will remain always, but I can't let them loose to dance around in my head. Not yet.

It was January of 1996. I was forty-nine years old and I'd wanted to learn how to dance around a ballroom for years. My ex-husband couldn't keep time, so if I wanted to dance, I always led. It made it difficult and embarrassing when a real dancer wanted me for a dance partner, because I proceeded to lead every man I danced with. I wanted to learn how to dance without bouncing around like I did in high school and learn to actually follow! So, when the local ballroom dance class started up through the park bureau, I was first in line.

Learning to dance properly was amazing. I'd already learned the Jitterbug, Foxtrot, Cha Cha, Waltz, Two Step and Rumba. The Tango? It was a test for me, but everyone laughed at everyone else and we all tried anyway. I'd been attending the singles dance class for three months. Newly divorced within the previous year, I knew dancing was the top of my 'single bucket list.' It was good exercise and the dancing community in Portland was friendly and enjoyable. There were a lot of dancers in the group and I'd dated a couple of the men from the class, but I had no interest in a serious relationship.

I was enjoying single life. No deadlines. I never had to call home if I was going to be late. Jumping in the car to drive anywhere, anytime with anyone was pretty darned exciting. And since I'd always loved music and dancing, life was very good. Find a man wasn't even a blip on my radar, but we all know when life throws you a curve ball, you'd better own a mitt.

It was Monday night and the music gently blasted from the CD player on the stage. Everyone lined up, anxious for class to begin. As the music filled the large room, our silver-haired ballroom instructor danced the two-step alone, while yelling, "1-2 back, 1-2 forward, 1-2 back and turn around." That's when I caught sight of the stranger in the class and his tidy copper beard.

Music changed and class began. I joined the ladies who circled the room as the men lined up inside our circle and proceeded to tap and sway in the opposite direction. We bumped along to the jazzy tune until the music stopped abruptly. The man who stood motionless in front of me was my dance partner.

"1-2 back, 1-2 forward, 1-2 back and turn around," bellowed above the music and I matched my partner's steps, covertly twisting my head to watch the red-bearded stranger. When I saw his hand lift reddish-grey hair off his forehead, I smiled across the room. And then wondered how I could finagle to be in front of him when the music broke into the change-a-partner routine again.

When Red Beard got closer during the next set, I chickened out. Being single again was still new. And being apprehensive, I avoided socializing with strange men. The music changed to country western; he and his partner danced in my direction. It was the best music for the two-step; the stranger had perfect timing and his dancing made my feet tap like a woodpecker stabbing the side of an old tree. Our eyes linked and he smiled. Red hair. Grey eyes. Nice smile. And interest.

The circle began again and I missed him by three partners. I kept smiling because I couldn't stop. I'd see his partner, and then he'd come into view, swinging her around like a pro. This time, I decided, shyness wasn't going to get in the way.

When the instructor called for a ten-minute rest, my girlfriend and I left the dance floor and reached for lemonade. A man I knew touched my elbow and asked me to save a dance for him later. I nodded, grinned

and turned around to find myself staring up into Red
Beard's face. With a surprised smile, I moved aside to
talk with friends but my mind wasn't on the
conversation.

When the music filled the room to invite us back onto
the dance floor, the instructor's voice called out, "Free
dance for the next fifteen minutes and then we'll do a
waltz before the end of class." Music blared and men
and women jostled to find partners.

I had just dropped my paper cup in the trash bin when I
felt a tap on my shoulder. Turning around, my eyes
opened wide to see Red Beard holding out his hand
toward me.

"Is this our dance?"

"Absolutely."

His name was James, aka J. D. He grinned and so did
I. We fit like a glove as he glided me onto the center
of the dance floor and led me into a jitterbug to the
tune, "In the Mood." He could dance! Fifteen minutes

slid by in a heartbeat. I wasn't ready for the class to begin again. He intrigued me, as I'd never dated a man with a beard before. In fact, I'd never liked beards. That night in class, I changed my tune (pun intended) and I'd said yes to a dinner date.

Within the next three years, we dated, danced, travelled and married. The song at our wedding was, of course, "Can I Have this Dance for the Rest of my Life" by Anne Murray. He took me away from Portland all the way east to Williamsburg, Virginia where we found a fixer-upper house near the Chickahominy River in Charles City. I hardly knew where Williamsburg was on the map before we married, but that's where J.D. had been born and raised and that's where he wanted to retire. I loved traveling, so off we went.

When I said, "I do" and jaunted 3,000 miles away from my family, I left the big city for a little house in the woods. I learned to garden, helped build a deck, named resident bluebirds "Maude and Harold" and watched them flit in and out of their new bird house. I planted, weeded, watered and planted some more. I learned about Mayflies, Japanese beetles, voles, humidity, cicadas, snakes, raccoons, and bugs of all sizes. I couldn't open my screens for fresh air because of insects called 'no seeums' for obvious reasons; they slip through window screens. I painted an Arabian carpet on the new deck outside our sliding doors; projects were never ending and I still maintained my day job for my Oregon employer through cyberspace. From dancing the jitterbug in Oregon to learning to water-ski in Virginia, I felt the excitement of dancing across the boat wake and along the shores of our river. It was mind-boggling. First there were two skis. I learned quickly to get my butt up and out of the water because the repercussions were too nasty to discuss. When he told me I should kick off a ski and slide across the water on one, I looked at him like he was nuts.

"You can do it," he yelled.

"Why should I want to?" I yelled back.

I couldn't kick away one ski because when I tried it, I fell from hell to breakfast and I gulped down half the Chickahominy River. A bruise the size of my head rose on my inner thighs and I thought my shoulders were ripped from their sockets. So, plan B was using one ski to begin with. He bought me a slalom ski. And I did it! Over fifty and there I was skiing down the river and jumping over wakes behind our Mastercraft boat. It was as good as dancing. During our years on the river, I created too many gardens; one for birds filled with birdbaths, a water feature and bird houses, roses, and a small Merlot vineyard. A southern Magnolia added charm among the dogwood trees and centred the landscape. But I'd created a monster and couldn't keep up with the weeds. J.D. cleared acreage, planted grass, and bought a riding lawn mower.

Our dancing days were over and my skiing days were too. The property owned us. Dancing is now a memory along with my gardens, his grass and our never-ending projects. Now, we live in Arizona where the sky is bright blue, palm trees sway above a pergola and life is easy. I exchanged my gardens for courtyard container pots and a laptop to write and write some more. J.D. exchanged his riding mower for a La-Z-Boy chair and a smart T.V.

Life was more than I expected the next chapter to be. His beard was no longer red and there was silver in my hair.

But if my husband's knees didn't scream, I know he would have still asked me, "Is this our dance?"

And I'd answer, "Absolutely."

For now, I pull the threads of the silver linings and find the hint of adventure in my newly adapted life. I can get up in the morning at my leisure, eat what and when

I want to, go shopping or visit friends without hurrying home. No timelines. Sometimes, hollowness pervades the stillness of the empty house when I return. Widowhood is nothing as I'd imagined it would be, but I am owning it and looking beyond the horizon as J.D. hoped I would. There is light at the end of this eternal tunnel that I glimpse a few times more often as the days pass by. There is always hope and I can still hear him say, "You need to get your mind right…" when I needed an attitude adjustment. I can smile now, hear his words and simply nod. Yes, getting my mind right is a considerable chore but each day when I wake up, I promise myself I will find one thing that gives me joy. I do not say it is easy, but it is definitely an attitude, a completely different way of life. For me, I carry all the memories inside to pull one or two out when I feel it's safe to do so. Yes, I still have crying moments. However, my smiles are coming more often and one day I hope to imagine his laughter and laugh along with him in my mind.

Yes, hope follows my footsteps and for other widows who are just learning what it really means to put one foot in front of the other, I applaud each day you can recognize and cherish the memories. Grieve as you feel you must. Do not let anyone tell you how to grieve, when to grieve or not to grieve. You make the choice and take as long as you need. We are all sisters in widowhood and reaching out to others to help each other along our way can give us one of the daily joys I spoke of. Our widowhood success depends on making OUR choices on the grieving process, not the many options others dictate in their heartfelt and often impatient responses to our tears and vulnerability.

Taking baby steps from devastating widowhood-grief to the next chapter in my life has been slow and I try not to be too hard on myself. It has been a twisting, wrenching journey. The sadness was so great; I could not create the words to express the dislocation, the change, the stillness. I do not expect my grieving to let up any time soon but as I look back to that day, I know I have grown and will continue to do so. The heart thumping fear of being alone, the actual loneliness and the glimpse of life beyond hammers at me still, but I can now look at our photographs, fragrant with memories.

I truly believe that "Life isn't about waiting for the storm to pass. It's about learning to dance in the rain." I found this saying etched on a small piece of wood in an antique shop recently and when I read it, the words slapped me awake. I felt that thread of hope rekindled and I brought it home to read each day. I will be alive with life and create my own joy each day as I keep going on, taking those baby steps.

The silence still grows thick as fog some nights and aloneness surges over me. Heavy. Like the ocean waves whipping across the silver sand at the beach. Crosswinds of change buffet our every moment as those baby steps turn into strides just as a baby learns to walk. So shall I.

Chapter 3

Borderline.

By :Michael Whelan.

Eric Shipton, a British diplomat and adventurer
stationed in Kashgar at the end of WW2, heard about
an arch in a mountain range north of the city that was
so large it could be seen from 40km away. After three
unsuccessful attempts to reach it from the south, he
eventually did arrive at the magnificent arch from the
north with the help of a local guide. In his book The
Mountains of Tartany, 1947, Shipton introduced the
arch to the world.

Incredibly there are no accounts of anybody visiting
the arch for the next 53years.

In May 2000, a team, sponsored by the National
Geographic, set out to locate, climb and survey the

legendry arch in Xinjiang Province in the far west of China.

When the December 2000 edition of the National Geographic Magazine arrived at my desk, featuring an account of the expedition and confirming that at almost 457 meters, it is indeed the tallest known natural arch in the world, the seed was sown and I knew at that moment I would visit the arch some day.

Why did I want to see it? I'm not sure if I can answer that. I'm tempted to say "Why not"? When I make a decision to take on an expedition I can be blindly positive in my approach, enthusiastic, confident, and if I ever do experience self-doubt, it usually evaporates if I utter the mantra "If you think you can, you will". I wasn't surprised, but I was little concerned by the reaction on social media, especially when I posted my intended route and announced it would be a solo trip.

In my defence I must say this was not the first unusual journey or solo trip I had undertaken.

.

The first thing you notice when you open an atlas is that, although Kashgar is in the Peoples Republic of China, it is so far west that it is almost halfway between Europe and Beijing. Actually a pillar south of Kashgar in Tashkurgan proclaims, (one of many such claims), that this is the half way point on the Silk Road.

The most obvious way to get to Kashgar from Europe would be to fly to Beijing and take a domestic connection via Urumqi. Now let's see if I could make that journey a little more interesting. Fly from Dublin to Islamabad in Pakistan. Then cycle the Karakoram Highway "KKH" from Islamabad to Kashgar, 1300km of mountain road, taking in the views of the Himalayas, the Karakoram and the Pamir Mountain ranges. Now add the world's highest border crossing, the Khunjerab Pass 4700m. Using Kashgar as my base, I would visit the arch before taking a four-day train journey across China before flying home from Beijing. Certainly not everybody's cup, glass or bowl of tea, but for me, the stuff adventures are made of.

During my research in exploring various ways of making the trip to Kashgar, I discovered the city was a major crossroads on the Old Silk Road, with an ancient southern spur route leading through the Pamir and Karakoram mountains into modern day Pakistan. This route is now the subject of massive financial investments from both Pakistan and China due to its strategic importance in providing a road link between western China and the port of Karachi and the Arabian Sea. Some of the major obstacles on this route, apart from the security situation in Pakistan, are the difficulties associated with extreme weather at high altitude, rock fall and landslides. That's not all; the area is also prone to earthquakes. However this has not deterred both countries in pressing on with the project. Nor me with mine!

My journey would take about 6 weeks. Training started with the purchase of a Trek 21 speed-touring bike in August 2015. It was many years since I did any cycling and even longer since I did any bike touring. The bonding was instant. After an initial one-hour early morning spin around the hills of Dunmore East in Co Waterford, I was wondering why I had not cycled for so long. Over the course of the next eight months, as part of my training, I would cycle about 300km per week. Planning the trip came easy and was something I enjoyed, buying bits and pieces that were needed along the way, ordering maps of the Karakoram Highway from Stanfords in London, reading Jonathan Tuckers, The Silk Road, again and again. I kept up to date with the political and security situation in Pakistan and researched the history of the Uyghur people in western China. As the time approached came the joy of going to Dublin to get my Pakistani and Chinese visas.

The build up is an important part of any expedition. However not everything can be prepared for, many things are well outside of our control including extreme unseasonal weather, political and security situations and so on. The attack on the army public school in Peshawar on 16th December 2014 in which 132 children and 9 staff members were killed was a game changer in Pakistan. Since then the Pakistani authorities have declared all-out war on the Taliban, reintroducing the death penalty and carrying out more than three hundred executions in 2015. With many Taliban members in prison awaiting trial, the risk is obvious to westerners. The struggle of the Pakistani authorities to maintain law, order and control, combined with a resistance and pushback from Islamic extremists who are prepared to use violence, has had a pernicious effect on much of the country. It has even forced the Pakistani cricket team to play all its home internationals outside Pakistan. Depending on which website you visit, the travel advice for Pakistan varies. The US Government warns U.S citizens against all travel to Pakistan. The U.K Government advises against travel in the tribal areas, Quetta, Baluchistan, and Peshawar and on the Karakoram Highway between Islamabad and Gilgit. Looking at that positively, I read that the Karakoram Highway is safe to travel north of Gilgit.

Embassies have changed so much since I made an overland trip to the Himalayas in 1979. Back then you could write to an embassy, tell them you wanted to visit their country and a few days later a big brown envelope would arrive with maps and information on places of interest. If you wrote to an embassy now you would probably be red flagged and put on a security list. Phoning an embassy is even more difficult. If you are lucky enough to speak to a real person they will probably tell you to go onto their website. My first contact with the Pakistani embassy in Dublin was on a beautiful early spring morning in Aylesbury Road.

The visa section is located in an out building to the rear of the embassy. There were about a dozen people in the queue mostly of Pakistani origin. Those arriving at the embassy were told by an attendant to take a ticket and wait for their number to appear on the screen. One gentleman who refused to take a ticket, (I assumed he felt much too important), was asked, "What are you, some kind of tough guy?" I can't imagine that happening in the Chinese embassy. A sign there simply reads "SILENCE".

The cost of visas is an issue for me. I paid over €170 for my Pakistani and Chinese visas. In the past they were often free, or just a nominal charge applied. Also the visa section in the embassy is now more than likely to be located away from the embassy proper in the equivalent of the garden shed or through the tradesman's entrance. My worst to date has to be the Mongolian embassy in Beijing. Visa applicants are forced to stand on the public footpath and communicate through a one-way glass window in the embassy wall. Overall there is plenty of room for improvement in the attitude shown towards visa applicants by embassy staff. Not all of us are drug smuggling terrorists, and no, we don't want to corrupt your citizens and overthrow your government. We just want to visit your country spend some money and enjoy ourselves. So be nice to us and by the way €30 for a one month visa is enough. Glad I got that off my chest.

April 24th 2016. Visas intact, bike dismantled and packed into a large cardboard box, and airline ticket printed, destination Islamabad. The 18-hour stopover with Turkish Airways in Istanbul was welcome. I booked a small apartment close to Sultan Humid in the city centre. Very few tourists about for the time of year. I paid a nostalgic visit to the Pudding Shop of Midnight Express fame and the Grand Bazaar. There were Syrian refugee children selling paper tissues outside the Blue Mosque, and anglers still fishing off Galata Bridge. I had an interesting talk with a man in the tourist office about Gallipoli. It was the 101st anniversary. He was not a fan of Winston Churchill to say the least. He was also very angry over the recent bombings in Istanbul and the effect it is having on the whole tourist industry. Istanbul is a pleasure to visit. There is so much to see that I constantly promise myself to come back and spend more time. I enjoyed being a tourist for the day, before checking out the new metro on my way to Ataturk Airport for my evening flight to Islamabad.

Even the name Benazir Bhutto International Airport evokes memories of assassination and violence. When I arrived at 3am I didn't want to leave the airport. I went straight to the PIA counter to book a domestic flight to Gilgit, a city where, according to my research, the security situation begins to relax and it is relatively safe for foreigners. No such luck! The next available flight was in 10 days time. Pakistan had experienced unprecedented rainfall for much of March and early April resulting in the Karakoram Highway being blocked at more than 200 locations as a result of rock fall, mud and landslides. The disruption to the KKH had caused a huge demand for tickets on the twice-daily flight. The situation was so serious that food and medicine shortages were starting to occur in villages along the way. Then I discovered it was possible to take a private car from outside the airport as small vehicles were making it through to Gilgit. "You can be there in fifteen hours," said the agent. This was the section of the KKH that the UK government specifically advised against travelling - decisions, decisions. Would I take a chance and go by private car, or hang around Islamabad for ten days? Within half an hour I had done a deal with an agent, my bike and gear were in the back of a car as the two drivers and I headed north though the suburbs of Islamabad.

 The first roadblock we came to was calm enough until one of the soldiers noticed me and shouted "foreigner". I love listening to Urdu with its blend of English. I'm sure there are many words for foreigner in Urdu, but they always seem to use the English version when referring to me. The situation at the roadblock went from casual, with identification cards being produced by the drivers and pondered over, to a sense of high alert when they discovered a foreigner onboard. This was the beginning of much form filling, "Passport number? Visa number? Where issued? Coming from?

Going where? Address in Pakistan? Purpose of visit? People you are meeting? Further along the highway I was photographed many times at check posts, though I'm not sure why. What happened next was supposed to make me feel safe. An armoured jeep arrived with five soldiers. "Ok, we will escort you". Up until late 2015 on this section of the KKH vehicles travelled in convoy with armed escort. Then in 2016 the security situation was reviewed and five thousand personnel were deployed to protect the highway and supply armed escort where required. I must say it did not necessarily make me feel safe driving behind an armed escort, especially when they would get impatient with the locals while driving through busy towns and put on the siren. This I felt was just drawing attention to me for a would-be assassin. We stopped in Abbotabad at a roadside café for breakfast as children made their way to school. Abbotabad is located about 100km north of Islamabad and was home to Osama Bin Laden until the CIA raid on his compound on May 2nd 2011. As I sat there sipping sweet Pakistani tea I was starting to think this is all a bit weird.

Because of the damage to the highway, the journey to Gilgit took about 26hours with much of it on detour roads. We had a change of guard many times along the way, with each group of armed guards not travelling more than about 40km or so. . The journey from Islamabad to Gilgit passes through the city of Challis and close to Nanga Parbat, the scene of the June 22nd 2013 base camp mass murder when eleven unarmed mountaineers from various countries were executed by a group of Taliban members dressed as Gilgit scouts. Their original plan was to take the mountaineers hostage, but something went horribly wrong and they were executed on that mid summer's day. Nanga Parb, at 8126m, and the beautiful Fairy Meadows were, up until then, very popular with trekkers and climbers. Sadly that industry does not exist any more.

We arrived in Gilgit early morning and I booked into the Shaheen International Hotel on Airport road. I must say the city was not a welcoming or attractive place on arrival. Even the Shaheen Hotel, with a stuffed Ibex in the foyer, and its 1970s décor, did nothing to enhance the situation. Next morning was a real shock. Whatever romantic notion I had about Gilgit being a calm and peaceful hill station, cool and away from the hustle and bustle of Punjab, was certainly not immediately apparent. From my breakfast table I could see a hole about the size of a golf ball in the window. Turning my head 180 degrees, there it was, an exit hole from a high velocity bullet leading into the courtyard of the hotel. The amount of military vehicles on the busy street outside caused me some concern. Then I noticed a large street poster of a young, smiling

83

Saddam Hussein taking pride of place on the city's main street. I decided to calm down and enjoy my breakfast go back to my room and assemble my bike. The paddle fans stop spinning as the power and wi-fi are switched off. A note at reception informed me, I was to report immediately to the police station to discuss my travel plans. Directly outside the hotel entrance was a concrete bunker, complete with sand bags and fully armed soldiers in bullet proofs and tin hats. I was the only westerner "Foreigner" staying in the hotel, and once again, when the troops saw me, they immediately stepped up a gear. It was as though their only purpose was to protect and accompany me to the station. At the police station I met a young plain-clothes officer and we chatted over several glasses of tea. He wasn't giving out too much information about the security situation further north on the KKH, only that his officers would provide an armed escort, as it was not safe to go any place outside my hotel alone, or travel by bicycle. Not quite what I had in mind.

Karimabad in the Hunza valley was my next destination, but this required travel by minibus or by private car with an escort. I'd had enough of private cars after that journey up from Islamabad, so I decided to opt for the minibus. It took some persuading for them to sell me the ticket. "Foreigner is problem for bus", the ticket seller kept repeating, which did not make me feel good. After much arguing with the officer I was issued with a ticket for a 7am departure the following morning. On my way back to the hotel I stopped at several ATM's, but none of them would accept my credit card. When I arrived back at the hotel with no electricity or wi-fi and no money, I began to feel very down. Things were not at all going to plan. The Karakoram Highway was still blocked with mudslides north of Sost, and they were having real difficulty trying to clear it. Food and medicine was being airlifted into isolated villages. The security situation was much more intensive than I had anticipated, and the likelihood of ever getting to China via the Khunjerab pass was looking increasing unlikely.

I think it was at that point I didn't want to be there any more. I was wishing I could be transported back to my bedroom in my house in Dunmore East, Ireland. I wanted normal things. I wanted to stroll along my local beach. I wanted to cut the grass in my garden. I wanted it to be Saturday morning and I wanted to be having breakfast with my wife and daughter. I want to go home now. I'll go back to Islamabad by road, book a flight home and call the whole thing off. It was a big mistake to even come here in the first place, why didn't I listen to all the subtle warnings from my Facebook friends like "Mind yourself, take care, come back safe", and the not so subtle ones like "Are you sure it's safe to go to Pakistan? Can you get insured for that trip? Don't they have ISIS there? Are you mad"?

My bike started to look ridiculous, my pannier bags started to look stupid, and I was much too old to be doing this trip. I'm so irresponsible wasting all those policemen and soldier's time, putting their lives at risk just to protect a tourist with a stupid ambition to cycle from Pakistan to China. Oh the negative thoughts were gushing through my head. Is this what it feels like to be going insane? I felt trapped. Going back was not a viable option, and the uncertainty of going forward was making me anxious beyond belief. The bike I spent eight months lovingly preparing for the trip was loaded up and ready to go and I could barley look at it. My self-confidence was so low the bike was becoming embarrassing. I just wanted to drape it with a big blanket and hide it away. I didn't sleep that night, but I did, somehow manage to dismantle everything from the bike and subconsciously make the decision to keep going.

As we left Gilgit for Karimabad, I had what was probably the scariest moment of my life, but it was also a turning point on my trip. A few miles outside the city we stopped at a police station, my escort left the bus and went inside. Shortly afterwards a man appeared across the road wearing a traditional navy shalwar kameez, (baggy pants & long loose shirt), with a small machine gun slung over his shoulder. He walked towards the bus and asked the driver who was the foreigner. What was going through my mind? I can remember exactly, and it was strange. I'm the guy who spent his life objecting to racist comments directed at Pakistanis. As I tried to stand with the back of my head pressed against the ceiling I was hoping he would shoot me in the chest and not in the face.   Just then he smiled and I noticed a rolled up beret tucked into his shoulder strap. He was of course my new police escort and not an assassin! A huge sigh of relief and suddenly everything started to look beautiful again. It may have been a combination of the relief from that dark negative place I was in my head, compounded with an unhealthy degree of paranoia, but from that moment my whole attitude towards the trip changed. The music on the bus radio sounded just right, my bike was the best bike in Pakistan, and I was going to cycle over the Khunjerab Pass into China without even feeling the effects of high altitude. Oh by the way, mudslides would not stop me now, I would just cycle through them.

As we made our way along the road towards Hunza the scenery became unbelievable with views of Mount Rakaposhi and Lady Finger. I booked into the Hunza View Hotel .A function had just finished in the hall.

Although Pakistan is governed by Sharia law, and therefore alcohol is not legally available, the large group that had just exited from the May Day celebrations were in high spirit. One man asked me my country then declared he was a worker, and May 1st was his day. There was something very positive and admirable about his attitude and approach. Here was a man in a country in political turmoil, being slightly defiant by consuming some home brew, and being in no doubt as to his identity. He was not a communist or a union official, "I'm a worker" he declared, and seemed so proud of that fact and of his day. That evening I was invited to a barbeque in the hotel garden, lots of innocent looking transparent liquid being consumed from even more innocent looking water bottles. All I'm saying is if you ever ran out of fuel for your car, or if you needed paint stripper, it might come in handy. I stayed in Karimabad for two days visiting the fabulous, but earthquake damaged,

Baltit Fort. This palace was occupied by the Mir's of Hunza for 700 years until it was abandoned in 1945 when the royal family moved to a new palace further down the valley. Following a restoration programme funded by the Aga Khan, and completed in 1996, the Fort is now a museum housing many of its original artefacts. Ultra Glacier cascading down from Mt Butura 7785m once offering a natural line of defence from the north, has now retreated some 3km back up the valley.

Cycling from Karimabad to Passu you soon cross a bridge over the Hunza River. About 5km along the road is the Sacred Rock of Hunza. Just in case there was any doubt that this was an important route on the Silk Road, the Buddhist, Christian, Hindu and Islamic carvings on the roadside rock prove that not only was this the route, but this exact location was an actual camping and resting area on the Silk Road. I was also reassured before leaving Karimabad that the explosions I was hearing late into the night were not some major battle taking place up the valley, but were the frantic efforts being made by the heroic road workers and the Pakistani army to clear the rock fall and keep the KKH open. Sometimes the damage to the highway is so enormous that it is beyond repair. In 2010 a massive landslide completely blocked the highway for 5 years, resulting in the creation of a very scenic 19km long lake at Attabad. Boats were used to ferry goods across the lake until a12km tunnel was bored through solid rock reconnecting the highway in 2015. Work is still in progress on a 7km section of the tunnel, with lighting and ventilation being installed. I was not allowed cycle through that section. Thanks again to the Pakistani police for transporting me and my bike through that long dark and dusty tunnel. Between Karimabad and Passu the road was blocked in many places, but nothing major. I had little difficulty getting through with my bike, but the trucks and busses had to wait until the large boulders were cleared. The mudslides were more difficult to deal with, a bit like trying to eat soup with a fork. This was what I came to Northern Pakistan for, cycling through these majestic valleys, the sound of gushing snow melt rivers. I really started to understand why this place was believed to be the fabled Shangri-La. The hotels in Passu were very quiet with almost all tours cancelled because of the highway damage. A sigh of relief for the wildlife as this area, being just outside the Khunjerab national park it is very popular with wealthy trophy hunters.

Cycling from Passu to Sost I started to notice the altitude but the scenery provided a welcome distraction. A group of small schoolboys ran next to my bike, some pushing me along the way. Like all schoolchildren, they looked smart in their school uniforms, even if some hadn't quite grown into their older brothers shoes. Sost is a high altitude busy border town where you must clear Pakistani customs before continuing the final 30km to the Chinese border at Khunjerab. Unless you can produce a polio vaccination cert you will not be allowed into China. Pakistan and Afghanistan are the only two countries left in the world where polio hasn't been completely eradicated. Sadly the polio eradication programmes are facing difficulties in both countries with recent deadly attacks on clinics in Kabul and Karachi. Apparently the Taliban believe that the eradication programme is some kind of sinister plot by the West. Khunjerab Pass, at 4693m, is the highest international border in the world. Foot passengers or cyclists are not allowed through, you must travel with a special licensed transporter. Some tourists travel up to the border from the Pakistani side on day trips just to take a look. The switchback hairpin bends and canyons along the KKH between Sost and Khunjerab are extraordinary, and you really do wonder how anybody could possibly have built such a road. With my polio vaccine in order, sprayed for Dengue fly, and X-Rayed until my fingertips tingled, I was safely through the Khunjerab pass and into China.

Arriving in the first Chinese town, Tashkurgan, I booked into the K-2 Hostel. This was a good place to meet a few westerners and get some up to date information. Most of the people at the hostel were surprised, and some amazed, that I had come into China from Pakistan. They had made the journey by air from Beijing to Kashgar, with the majority of them actually living and working in China. Strolling around Tashkurgan next morning I really noticed the cultural difference between this part of China and Pakistan. Although the Uyghur population is predominantly Muslim, there is a strong Han Chinese influence, which is very much encouraged by Beijing. The women are brightly dressed and look a little like dolls with their flick out skirts wool tights, cylinder shaped hats draped with transparent scarves, and glitzy handbags. The men were a bit of a let down, looking much duller in their ill-fitting suits, but some did wear colourful hats. I walked into a vast venue in the centre of town and sat for half an hour watching dancers rehearse. It was culture dancing and I couldn't believe how similar it was to traditional Turkish dancing. When I heard the language being spoken in a teashop later that morning I thought I had arrived in the wrong country. Many of the words are pronounced, as you would hear in Istanbul or Ankara.

The scenery as I cycled through from Tashkurgan to Kashgar was beyond anything I had imagined. Even with the forever changing landscape, Mount Muztagh 7534m and Mount Kongur 7720m dominated the skyline for much of the three-day cycle. The incredibly beautiful Karakuli Lake, with nomadic yurt dwellers, and yak herders made this part of China looks more like Tibet meets Mongolia. Looking at some of the yurt dwellers features, .I wasn't surprised to hear that they have their origins in Mongolia. I stayed with a family next to the lake with a yurt all to myself, complete with evening meal and breakfast before cycling downhill all day through the canyons of the Pamir Mountains. The scale of the road works on this section of the KKH will change the highway forever. To protect the highway from rockfall and landslide, the Chinese have decided to raise huge sections of the road onto massive concrete columns, high above the canyon floor. I estimated these road works went on for between 80 and 100km. The canyon cnds abruptly with the road works about a day's cycle outside Kashgar, and from there the going is flat and easy, as the landscape becomes more densely populated and urbanised.

Kashgar, a major crossroad on the Silk Road and still home to one of the oldest animal markets in Asia, was much larger than I expected. My first impression as I approached the ancient city, which represents the end of the KKH, was that I was now running with the herd, surrounded by dozens of cyclists, and silent electric scooters at every junction. I was now blending in and becoming less of an object of curiosity. As we waited for the countdown indicator to turn green at the many traffic lights, the smiles from the pillion passengers, usually a young woman sitting side -saddle and carrying a child in her arms, made me feel welcome. This could be anywhere in the world with its modern high-rise offices and up market hotels complete with extravagantly grand entrances. But thankfully, just like Marrakech, the old city is protected, preserved and very much alive and intact. It was a joy to stay for almost a week, exploring the ancient streets and markets before taking on my final challenge, a cycle and hike and campover to Shipton's Lost Arch. The arch is only about 100km north of Kashgar but is uphill most of the way. Setting out early morning I stopped for breakfast and lunch in some interesting villages along the way. After about 7 hours of cycling I thought I had reached the location of the arch only to find out I had another 16km of uphill road to travel, and a one-hour hike and climb. After leaving the main road I only met one person. That was like a trip back in time. He had his hair in a man bun. He was carrying a large bamboo birdcage with what looked like a Pheasant or Himalayan Snowcock inside. He was a bird catcher and demonstrated to me how he would cast his net over curious wild birds that came too close.

Shipton's Arch now has a visitor's centre that closes at 18:00. When I arrived at 18:15, not wanting to be refused entry, and told to come back next day, I hid my bike, removed my pannier bag containing some food and water, and continued the final journey towards the arch on foot. It was a dull evening with a lot of cloud. Actually the advice I got in Kashgar was not to go there alone in case I got lost. It's at times like this I am glad of my navigation skills. As I approached the arch the landscape started to look very familiar. I had looked this place up so many times online, I was starting to recognise the footbridges and rope ladders that make access to the arch inclusive. Then just before darkness fell, it came into view. No camera or photograph can do justice to the scale of this arch. The Empire State Building would fit underneath it, and I had it all to myself. As I set up my ground mat and my bivouac it started to rain. Just a soft light rain, the stuff we get a lot of in Ireland. It didn't bother me in the slightest. The arch was still clearly visible even after dark. Anyway I had bivouacked out in much more extreme conditions. I woke several times during the night and looked down to where the foot of the bed would normally be. Then with a smile on my face I would look at the sky, which by now had cleared, and was visible through and above the arch, I awoke early next morning feeling elated with an enormous sense of achievement.

 The journey back to Kashgar was almost entirely down hill. As I freewheeled along the road, I was reflecting on my journey up from Islamabad, what an adventure it had been. The intense security along the KKH south of Gilgit, the incredible beauty of the Hunza valley, the stupendously high border crossing at Khunjerab, and the wild landscape on the road from Khunjerab to Kashgar. I also reflected on the fear and paranoia I had overcome in Gilgit, and I remembered conversations I had with an old hiking friend about mental health, and how nobody is immune from hovering or dipping below that borderline. We all at some time in our lives, probably more often than we realise, pay that place a visit.   I suppose the important thing is we don't get stuck, and stay there for too long. My borderline along the KKH was not in an oxygen starved customs building at 4700m on the Khunjerab Pass, but somewhere between a hotel bedroom in Gilgit and a minibus ride to the beautiful Hunza Valley.

The End.

.

Chapter 4

Time for tea.

An Egyptian-Irish tale

By: Aisling Meath

Last night I had a dream. I was standing at the ocean. He rose from a green blue wave, came towards me and took my hand. He held me as we descended deeper and deeper into the foamy salty water. We swam inside glittering underwater palaces. We danced with mermaids, gliding up and down laughing and swaying in the buoyant waters. Shimmying down the great hall of mirrors, iridescent sparkles bouncing the light in every direction we drifted laughing and splashing. Entwined we swam towards the dazzling white light deeper and deeper. We met the great giant squid that gazed at me with his enormous kind eye. He spoke. His voice, like waves booming and murmuring, both loud and soft. The velvet moonlight penetrated deep darkness and was reflected in his eye, which looked like the entire universe was contained within.

" As above, so below" he said, and I wondered what he meant.

I turned to look at my husband but all I could feel was his grip loosening from around my waist and he was drifting off into the brilliant white light. I couldn't swim fast enough to keep up with him. I screamed for him to come back but all I could see was his face pale and helpless and his beautiful enormous brown eyes full of terror drifting further and further away from me. The current carried me upwards and away from the light and I found myself drifting alone on a vast grey ocean.

When I awoke my eyes were burning, my pillow soaked with tears. I looked at the place where my husband used to lie and remembered that he had drowned.

Shortly after the nightmare period something terrible happened close to where I lived.

On the 12th January 2012 fishing vessel named the "Tit Bonhomie" sank off Adam's rock in Union Hall West Cork, Ireland. Five fishermen drowned, their bodies were missing. Three men were from Egypt and two from Ireland. They were Michael, Wael, Shaban, Kevin, and Saied. One Egyptian man, Abdou, survived clinging to a nearby rock where he was later rescued. The body of his brother Wael was lost.

It took 21 days to recover all the bodies from the sea. The local community got busy and their first thoughts were to retrieve the bodies and return them to the grieving relatives.

 Official sea and rescue operations were put into place, and members from the sea fairing communities all over Ireland came with their boats, and their divers volunteering their services. Women placed flowers upon makeshift tables at the pier in Union Hall waiting. They made Egyptian food, Irish food, tea coffee soup and sandwiches to offer to the volunteers and those from the rescue services.

Hot food and support warmed the searchers through the bitter cold January days that followed. Local families opened their hearts, their homes and their time to the grieving relatives who waited around the pier looking lost and shocked. I waited with them too, my heart wrenched open, exposed and bleeding for them, and for myself as well. How could I offer them hope, when I had none to offer? My own husband, a fisherman, had been lost at sea, his remains never found. I looked at the jewel green beauty of the ocean, and in that moment I hated it.

The National Press gathered at the pier to report on the events which were unfolding. I saw journalists with tears in their eyes, cameramen who wished they could look the other way when mothers came to wait for the bodies of their sons.

The local newspaper "The Southern Star" asked me to write an account of what it was like during those dark days of heartbreak and loss.

Here is that account:

"There are times when there are just no words. As I stood on the pier at Union Hall this past week for sunset prayers the raw emotions were palpable. The warm and generous people of West Cork and the Egyptian community from all over Ireland stood united in grief as we prayed for the recovery of the bodies of five fishermen lost off the sunken vessel the "Tit Bonhomme."

We watched and waited as yet another trawler came in after another fruitless search.

A flock of noisy seagulls were swarming in its wake, their flight illuminated by the lights of the back of the boat. Their squawking and the sound of the ebb and flow of the tide both taunted and soothed us. Over that the only other sound was the murmuring of the Catholic rosary, calling to Mary Mother the Star of the sea. Then the Koran prayers drifted over the sound of the waves invoking God. Allah Allah, if it is your will please please return the bodies to us. Inshallah Inshallah. If it is God's will. The sound was haunting, the fervour profound.

The recovery of some of the bodies was a poignant relief. At the same time, a double-edged sword. It was so heart breaking to have these fine young men being returned to us dead, when they should be alive. Yes-I'm going to say it. So unfair and so cruel. A waste of beautiful life. Yet we were so grateful to get their bodies, but heartbroken for the waiting relatives who's loved ones had not yet been found.

I remember another time, almost two years ago now, standing on that same pier gazing out to sea. My own lovely husband, an Egyptian fisherman, Nadi Sehsaah, (known as Nadir), was lost off the boat the "Janiriah" near the Fastnet Rock in Roaring Water Bay. He was thirty- three years old. The hope of finding his body diminished fast. After a few days the search was called off, and I had to come to terms with the fact that there was little hope. Again, at that time I was sustained by the warmth and generosity of the people of West Cork. It was what kept me going. I will always be grateful for the support that was shown to me, and will never ever forget it.

I remember Nadir saying to me; "I always sleep well in the sea." Those words often come back to me now. He is asleep in the sea. It is an Islamic belief that when a man dies at work, he goes straight to God. I nurture the hope that if he had time to realise what was happening and that he was not going to make it,

that knowledge would help him surrender. We live in hope. But we never really know.

In October 2010 I went to the village of Borg Meghezel in Egypt, to visit my husband's family. We had been married a year before he died in the Mosque according to Islamic tradition, and then at the registry office only two weeks before he died. We were planning a big Egyptian wedding with all our families gathered together in his village in October. But when October came I went alone with my son.

Borg Meghezel is located on the north coast of Egypt, near Alexandria, where the Nile meets the Mediterranean. Across the Nile, nearby, there is town called Rashid, (Rosetta), where the Rosetta stone hails from. The village resounds with a cacophony of sounds. Chickens clucking on the flat topped houses, and laughing children playing in the dusty streets transporting me back to another time, to the Dublin of my childhood, where there were always hordes of children playing hopscotch and skipping in the streets. The sound of the muezzin calling the prayers (Adhan) five times a day took a bit of getting used to, especially the one at sunrise.

Generations of these villagers are fishermen. It is the main industry, and the subsequent heartbreak of loss at sea is a way of life. As I write, and as this tragedy unfolds in Union Hall there is a fishing boat missing

from that same village, with fifteen people lost.
Nobody knows what happened to it.

The fishermen who come from there to Ireland, are
vastly experienced, skilled at net mending and some of
them have been at sea since they were nine years old,
as was the case with my husband. Visiting a place like
that, you realise that not everybody has the benefit of
an education, but if you are willing to work hard and
provide for your family you can make your way in the
world. Whatever it takes. The work ethic is strong in
the Egyptian culture. Many of the men who come to
Ireland send back money to support their families,
including their mothers and also their sisters if they are
not married. No woman is expected to fend for herself.
It is not the way. The men in Egyptian society take
their responsibilities as providers very seriously. The

family unit is very strong; nobody ever has to cope alone.

Again it is hard to put into words the depth of feeling and emotion, which met me in Borg Meghezel. Although it was heart breaking to come alone and with no body, at the same time it was so healing to cry and mourn with my new family, Nadir's brother's sisters and relations. They are a warm and hospitable people and both my son and I were welcomed not just by my in-laws but also by the whole village. Beautiful children followed us in the street laughing and calling out " I love you" "What is your name?" in an attempt to practice their English. Holding hands with the children we did feel loved there.

This past week my thoughts have been so much with the families of the Egyptian fishermen so far away waiting for news. The bridge leading into Borg Meghezel has been busy, as people have been gathering, waiting and praying. The scene at the pier in Union Hall is being echoed in Egypt. Reminiscent of an Irish wake, women are wearing black and mourning keening and crying aloud to Allah to bring them back, to give their families their remains to cry and pray over.

I remember walking up the street in the village and hearing somebody call my name. It was Wael Mohamed, and he was smiling running down the street after me. He was wearing a white galabia (long tunic robe), coming from his prayers in the mosque. He was back home for a holiday from fishing in Ireland to see his young wife and family.

His body was retrieved from the sea last Sunday. His brother Abduo, the only survivor of the wrecked trawler will accompany his remains to Egypt, where he will make the return journey home forever. May he rest in Peace. In my minds eye I will always see him that day in Borg Meghezel, his home place and happy in the sunshine. Tragically he never got to hold his two-month-old son and only saw him on the Internet.

As I write this the remains of Skipper Michael Hayes and Saied aly Eldin, only 24 years old have still not been recovered. I watch the sea with Saied's mother Aziza. Raised hopes then shattered again, like the waves crashing as another body is recovered and it is still not her curly haired boy.

Inshallah Inshallah. If it is God's will. .... In Union Hall and Borg Meghezel the people continue to wait and to pray. And to live in hope.

Rest in peace Michael Hayes, Kevin Kershaw, Shaban Attia, Wael Mohomed, Saied aly Eldin, Nadi Sehsaah and lost fishermen everywhere.

(Aisling Meath, Southern Star)

Aziza eventually retrieved the body of her son Saied from the sea. It was a Friday morning and she had come to the pier to pray looking out at the ocean and hoping that today would be the day. It was. I would not wish her pain on any mother. He was the last one to be found, but such is the gratitude of the mourner to be able to place flowers on a coffin and say goodbye. All the bodies were found, all the relatives able to have a funeral. Everyone got back to whatever they were

118

doing before all this tragedy, but everybody had changed.

One month later human remains were found in the area where Nadir was drowned. After months of DNA checking they were verified as his. I buried them according to Islamic tradition in the Muslim plot in a graveyard near Cork. The sea had claimed the rest of his body, but somehow all of this felt right. I was glad; it seemed like an ending point, a rest. I suppose that it was closure.

The world has changed totally since his death in 2010. The Egyptian revolution happened in 2011 and I remember looking at a crescent moon and thinking how amazed he would be at what was happening in his country, seeing it unfold on TV, on Facebook, on Twitter.

The ugly face of Islamaphobia has reared its head in the West, but people just want to be left alone and live in peace.

In times of heartbreak we recognize and respect each other's humanity. During those cold January days of 2012, on the pier in Union Hall there was no religion, no race, no colour, and no division. During those days people only recognized each other as mothers, fathers, sons and daughters, brothers, sisters. On that pier during those days people were just people.

If we look beyond the sensationalist stories we can realize that everyone, Muslim, Christian, Egyptian, Irish and beyond, loves nothing better than to sit together drink tea and swap stories. We all want to enjoy life.

So put the kettle on. Make tea not war.

I dreamed some more of gardens with green trees swaying in the breeze. Bees were buzzing among flowers of a thousand colours. We were all there, we were all laughing.

Chapter 5

PERMISSION TO HEAL AND THE PURPLE GIFT BAG

A CHAPTER IN MY GREAT LIFE JOURNEY

By: Madeline Page

When I consider my story, I think where do I start and what a great story. So many chapters, it's as if I've lived many lives. This particular chapter has inspired me to share my experience and encouraged me to finally put pen to paper, so here I am in the hope that this chapter of my life will shine some light to others.

On taking time to reflect, I'm starting this chapter from September 2014 as this was the time when physical symptoms I was having for quite a while started to

123

escalate and become more acute. Extreme tiredness, strong feeling of inflammation in my body, severe sweats, chest pain, insomnia, unhappiness, a feeling that was so unfamiliar to me as I had enjoyed great health and wellness throughout my life. I found myself to be at a crossroads asking myself how do I go forward.

Christmas came and although I was feeling unwell, there was no medical evidence of anything seriously wrong. I went through Christmas, making Christmas dinner for the family but found my body to be under a lot of pressure. Into the New Year and every new year I loved to focus on intentions for that year and would spend time reflecting and writing what I would love to achieve and focus on. This was the first New Year that nothing came to mind of 'doing'; I sat and waited feeling unsure of myself...

After a short time all that came into my mind was "ALL YOU NEED IS LOVE" I wrote this down in my little book over and over again. There was no feeling of doing something new, or improving aspects of my life that I had always focused on for the New Year. In a way it felt like I was shutting down, feeling my body was no longer a part of me, my mind unclear, unfocused, somehow dispirited. What was happening to me? and yet the message coming from deep within me was so strong and so clear, "ALL YOU NEED IS LOVE", is this what I was to pay attention to this year...

The symptoms got more acute and on the morning of the 8th of January as I washed my teeth I noticed an unusual lump on the side of my neck, more presented two days later. Starting to feel concerned and totally in the 'unknown' as to what was going on in my body I went to my doctor. On examining me he advised that I go directly to A&E. Lorcan, my wonderful husband, was with me all the way reassuring me that I was being looked after and everything would be OK.

I sat through A&E for over 24hrs focusing on my breathing and trying to stay calm. I was in the waiting game. Using my years of Yoga breathing and relaxation practice was amazing as I was able to sit through the waiting game with such physical discomfort and somehow I was still able to access a calm relaxed place inside myself. After lots of tests and seeing different doctors through the night, at 11am the following morning I was finally admitted to hospital with suspected lymphoma. It didn't register with me what was happening or even what a lymphoma was. I was just so relieved that finally after feeling so unwell for so long someone confirmed what I knew, something wasn't right. I was in a very unfamiliar place within myself but I was not alone, besides Lorcan there with me I somehow felt an extraordinary support with me all the time.

The relief of now being checked so thoroughly by experts in their field somehow allowed me to relax

126

even more and go with the process of more and more tests. I made the most of my time between all the tests by enjoying 'picnics' on the trolley with my wonderful sister Mary and good friend Dee who visited often and they were both so fantastic at keeping me positive and light. They were so good to me, bringing in lovely juices and warm smiles; there was always a laugh to be had. After spending two days on a trolley in the corridor I was finally given a bed in the ward, whoopee!!! I was sooo delighted. I treated it like a spa holiday, time and space to myself, to really see what's going on in my body and within my life - Somehow I felt my life was on hold. It was time to have a closer and deeper look at my life, something had to change. Dee brought me beautiful gifts of body creams and lotions that I indulged my body with, just as you would in a spa.

Lorcan and my two beautiful daughters always bringing comfort and reassurance to me. I spent the next three weeks apart from all the tests I had to undergo, relaxing, meditating, journaling and sleeping a lot. The first night in the ward was difficult for me in that I didn't sleep very well, and when I did, I had nightmares. I mentioned this to my magical sister so she could request a result/prayer for me through my good friend Tony who is a natural healer and master in mind technology and works on absent healing, with many wonderful results over the years I felt totally looked after. He was already aware where I was and was truly focused on healing on my behalf.

Well... the next morning I awoke as if I hadn't moved in the bed, somehow I had forgotten how that felt, it felt amazing, I was really rested, the first time in ages that I had slept through the night. Bernadette in the bed across from me said "oh my God what were you on last night, I'd love some of it". She went on to tell me that I roared with real belly laughter through out the night, not just giggles but real belly laughs. I was throwing my legs up in the air and across the bed, like I was watching the best comedy movie ever. Her description had me speechless as I honestly felt I hadn't moved in the bed and had the best sleep in a long time. Bernadette's bemusement and comment "where would you get it? certainly not here in a cancer ward, oh I'd love some of what ever you're on" left me so reassured that I was being truly looked after in the best and deepest way possible. The magic was really working. I had life and all its goodness on my side and somewhere deep inside of me I knew real LAUGHTER was something I truly had and needed more of.

The following two and a half weeks were spent under going lots of daily tests. I spent time in meditation every day and continued to write in my journal. I kept asking all that was not of me, the dis-ease to show it's self fully, no more hiding, it was time to be fully seen and it was OK to be seen. This conversation with my body began to show up with very clear results of what was actually going on but still to be confirmed by the doctors.

One of the days Ann in the bed beside the window eagerly wanted to know how to do a real relaxation, so I just asked her to join in with me. I started with focusing on my breathing and connecting to my body relaxing. Using my imagination I went on to have a walk by the sea in Malahide, seeing, hearing, smelling everything around me and becoming lighter, brighter, energised and much more relaxed as a result, all part of the real spa experience. Oh how I loved my imagination to bring up such wonderful states and how wonderful to work with my mind to connect to my natural state which is one of real wellness. For a short while I was free of my body's discomfort and savoured the feeling and the wonderful responses within my body. The ward felt calm and when I asked Ann did she enjoy her walk, she replied with such emotion how amazing it was for her. She couldn't believe the bodily and mind responses she got from doing the relaxation, she never experienced anything like it before. Ann hadn't walked for over three months due to an infection she got while on her treatment, so she had spent most of her time in bed. Walking in places she loves within her imagination was a whole new experience and brought up in her a motivation for her physio sessions to help speed up her recovery. My next little experience seemed to help her motivation to work more with her physio sessions, when she realised that how you think effects everything and where thought goes energy flows.

My blood pressure was reading very low, I was dizzy and my energy was extremely low. The nurse questioned how much I was drinking, that checked out OK. She then asked when was my last bowel movement, I had to really stop and think as I hadn't thought about it. What had a bowel movement got to do with it??? It had been three days but I had no feeling of constipation, no desire to have a bowl movement. She said she would have to intervene and went away to get some medication for me. Straight away I felt to lie on the bed, relax, go inside my body to see and feel for my bowel, of course my bowel is a part of me - but can I connect to it consciously, can I talk to it, would it respond? What happened next was amazing. I saw or got an impression of my bowel and it literally looked like a beautiful baby sleeping. I started to talk to it telling it how beautiful it is, what an amazing job it continually does for me, all the great work it has done for me and that it needs to WAKE UP now and continue its great work. Within 15mins I felt the urgent need to have a bowel movement. When the nurse returned I had no need for the medication and my blood pressure had returned to normal. This experience gave me a greater clarity and depth of acceptance of my mind body spirit connection and the miraculous responses with the right focus and debt of attention. I knew I needed to deepen my attention more to enhance my health and to connect more deeply with what heals my body. This experience gave me the opportunity to really connect and to explore the power of my own innate power within, the piece of God that I so believe to be my deeper self, the part that really heals, the "Super Me".

As more intensive tests were done it seemed that a clear diagnosis was being confirmed.

The day had arrived; the consultant had called myself and Lorcan into a private room. "Yes, you have Non-Hodgkin's Lymphoma, but it is very treatable although we can't cure it, yes you will lose your hair but more important is the prevention of infection". All I heard was I will lose my hair and they can't cure it, I broke down in that moment trying to digest it all. I realized how vulnerable I was as I was in shock and the doctor's words had a deep impact. Thank God in that moment that I quickly heard a prompt from deep within myself that they can't cure it medically, but that doesn't mean it can't be cured, the power of my own healing was to be truly explored.

Lorcan was my rock that day and the beautiful Maureen, my good friend who happened to travel all the way up from Galway to see me, they were amazing and so supportive in those initial diagnosis moments. The following few days were a blur as I was prepared for my first chemotherapy treatment....

Happy birthday Madeline, 3rd February, my 51st birthday. I had a special visit from my beautiful daughters Saoirse and Ashlinn, my wonderful husband Lorcan, my amazing parents and family, beautiful gifts, cards and a lovely lemon drizzle cake made by the magic Mags. All I could think was what a birthday gift, Chemo number 1, a real start to my healing, I was about to truly enter the unknown, with feelings of anxiety, though I knew the cure was deep within me. I had started my treatment. I had entered survival mode...

Non-Hodgkins Lymphoma, a type of cancer that affects the blood and lymph system which develops over time and in stages, and caused my immune system to slow down. My immune system was seriously compromised and with the chemo treatment, it was going to weaken even more. I knew my mind; body and spirit were designed to intervene with the dis-ease process at every point, including the chemo treatment. I accepted the chemotherapy was there to help in a physical way to prevent, slow down and reverse the disease and to help restore me so I could find my way back to my natural state of real health. This allowed me to face each treatment in an open way and work with the process I was now faced with.

Time to go home and return every 21 days for chemotherapy treatment...

It was three weeks since I slept in my own bed, it was so wonderful and a little scary to be back home again as I felt vulnerable and I knew I had yet to face more treatment and big changes. I didn't have clarity as to what the changes were but I knew some were in my home life. It really took time for me to adjust to being back home again but Lorcan and the girls made it as easy and as comfortable for me as possible. They were incredible and showed such love and care in every way, keeping me warm and as comfortable as possible. My amazing sister Mary continued to do the magic and organised the loan of an amazing juicer to get me the best nutrition. Both Mary and my magical daughters Saoirse and Ashlinn were my juicers giving me a daily, wonderful health regime of pure nourishment that came from my good friend Tony. I was in good hands and once again felt so looked after, cared for and loved by my awesome family and friends....

The following few weeks were filled with beautiful cards, flowers, presents and texts from so many people, some that I had never even met, friends of family. The abundance of Love and great goodness was over whelming in the best possible way. I felt so truly loved by my amazing family, dear friends, clients and even from people that I hadn't met, friends of friends and family, truly an amazing support. What an amazing capacity for Love that we all have!!! My environment became so completely stress free due to all this incredible support especially from my amazing family. I totally knew it was vital not to have any stress, as stress would compromise my ability to heal.

There were 'good days' and 'hard days'. The most challenging was the sickness and my very low energy and fatigue. As the chemo progressed I began to feel the cumulative effect more and more. My body had become more unfamiliar to me. Some nights I just couldn't sleep even though I was so tired, so fatigued.

One particular night while not been able to sleep as I felt the upset and the darkness of the treatment in my body, I made my way downstairs so as not to wake any of the family especially Lorcan who so needed his rest. I was becoming overwhelmed by the deep upset when I suddenly heard a good friend's voice in my mind. It was Mary B, a long time yoga client and friend of mine. Mary had sent me a wonderful card and in it she had said she always saw me as a great Warrior of Light. Through my tears I heard her say, "Remember, you are a WARRIOR OF LIGHT, you are a WARRIOR OF LIGHT". I literally 'stopped in my tracks', immediately I began to calm down and refocus my attention. My attention was now focusing on the warrior and light inside me and I found myself calling others to mind that I knew who believed in the light as being a powerful healing force. It was incredible how quickly I felt and saw the light get stronger and stronger within me, replacing the darkness. I felt so light, bright and a great sense of comfort filling all my cells and my whole being. This experience was a real reminder of wherever and whatever you focus your mind on 100%, there is a real response. Once again I got a prompt and felt the power of healing working it's magic in my mind and body. Even though physically I was alone in the sitting room, I felt such an overwhelming degree of support in the form of Love and remembered what I had written only some weeks ago, ALL YOU NEED IS LOVE. Returning to bed I soon fell into a real restful sleep, comfortable and reassured again that I was so looked after and so loved. I felt the presence of God all around me and within me so strong - I was never alone even in the depth of darkness that I so felt from the disease and chemotherapy drugs.

The Love that I was experiencing again and again was beginning to reveal to me the power of love at such a level and more of the power of healing was to be revealed.

 A few days later I got a wonderful invitation to come and sit for an hour or so with my good friend Arthur who is a natural healer and a group of fifty or so wonderful people who had gathered together. I was overwhelmed by the love and respect shown to me when I entered the room. I sat in the middle of the room with Arthur who introduced me with such acknowledgement, respect and love. The Beatles song "All You Need Is Love" was put on and every single person stood up and came up to me and made real contact of good wishes of health for me. It was sooo amazing and touched me in a way that was so profound I couldn't express it in words. I left the room after an hour or so feeling so powerfully loved and so grateful to every single person in that room and especially to the magical Arthur.

A few days later I got a card in the post from the lovely Carol, a friend who was at the healing weekend and it had a beautiful gift of a white wooden key with ALL YOU NEED IS LOVE written on it.

I began to see how this powerful sentence I had written back in January before my diagnosis was, the real lesson for me to learn in my life, a depth that I had yet to uncover and experience as this message was showing up again and again.

My dear friend Mags sat with me through my third chemo. As the nurses prepared the chemo, putting a purple bag over it to protect it from the light, a procedure they did every time with such precision and such care. We were both so relaxed, so present with what was happening. Mags held my hand, I could feel myself and Mags enter a real easy and very relaxed place, I could feel my energy as a warm glow going through me. When Mags said in her own beautiful way, "oh wow, how lucky are you, a PURPLE GIFT

BAG just for you..." I felt a shift in how I saw the chemo, I accepted in a deeper way the great job it was doing and how it was so precisely formulated for me. From then on that's how I saw each chemo treatment. It brought light to what could be seen as a dark experience. Mary and Mags were my main companions during Chemo as Lorcan had to continue with keeping our home and family running. Lorcan and the girls were truly amazing in how they kept everything so normal. We had lovely picnics of green juices and healthy goodies that the girls brought in and always brought the nurses over to check out and try for themselves. I was so blessed with such goodness and such magical people all around me. Even the nurses went out of their way to bring such comfort and fun to the hours spent getting chemo, true heroes, and real angels. The months went by slowly and I was told the cumulative effect of chemo is the hardest to come through. Physically that felt true but I knew the feelings of weakness and unfamiliarity would pass and I would find my way back to an even healthier me, my real natural state of health.

Six rounds of chemo, I'd done it!!! There was no trace of the disease and I was to continue with a lighter drug, Rituximab every 12 weeks for the next two years. Everyone was delighted and celebrating - I was relieved too but I wasn't celebrating. I couldn't connect with any feeling of celebration. I was stripped bare. In a way I felt so stripped bare of my whole life as I knew it, my hair was gone, my energy was gone; in a sense my whole purpose in life seemed forgotten. This was a scary place for me. I felt lost to my life as I knew it - how do I go forward? - Who am I now? How do I find my way back to my amazing healthy self and life?

I guess what I was facing now that the disease was under control was the permission to heal moment, from surviving to thriving. Real healing, all I need is love. My experience to date gave me the opportunity to shed light on and grow in places that I knew existed but I hadn't fully explored, working with the extraordinary power within me in an even deeper way than I had ever done before.

Permission to heal opened up a whole new depth of acceptance of my self and of my life. Could I really have compassion and real love for myself? .... Who and what I really am!!

Knowing that my body is a marvellous gift, I was given the space and time to really connect with it and to really listen to it. I asked myself the question, 'what are you here to teach me and how did I get to this point of dis-ease?'......

The following few months were the hardest for me as what I really, really needed to learn started to show it's self. Problems I was having in my personal life prior to my diagnosis and a general unhappiness of where I was in my life reared back up stronger than ever. All of it was put on hold emotionally, when I faced my diagnosis and chemo treatment. I began to explode with emotion, it felt like an over whelming avalanche. It seemed what I was now facing was even harder than the cancer diagnosis and treatment. There was so much trapped emotion, old resentments and grief and it ALL had to be released so real healing could begin.

I found my way to attend ARC an amazing support sanctuary in Ireland for anyone touched by cancer. It was through ARC and all the absent healing from Tony, Arthur, Aideen, my dear parents, my dear uncle Frank and my wonderful sister Mary that I found the support I needed to understand and enter the real healing journey.

Lorcan who was also unwell, and had been for a number of years, added to the trauma we were both experiencing as his illness was progressively getting worse. Both myself and Lorcan entered counselling through the support of ARC and my dearest uncle Frank, both of which helped guide us through the healing process. We both learned so much, especially about the impact of a trauma and especially unresolved traumas. We had both been through different traumas in our life together and never stopped to process and heal from them; this process was going to show up differently for both of us. Lorcan still had his own illness to process and fully heal from, and I still had to understand and accept that. The diagnosis of cancer was the one that stopped everything in its tracks for us both.

Now that I had come through treatment, I got the all-important nudge to look inward, deeper than ever before and to deal with the emotions and inaction I had somehow avoided for a long time. I wanted my life back and for it to be one of real health and happiness, to continue in a way that brought joy and real depth of learning and acceptance. It really was time to heal, to refocus on the life and goodness within each other, to see each others unique and beautiful light as we did when we first got together all those years ago, almost twenty six years ago. Getting caught in the traumas and issues, is what blinded us, covered us over and created the gaps that left us feeling we couldn't connect with our own selves, with each other and with life its self. The result for me was that I had developed real issues in my tissues/cancer.

I asked myself many questions and looked at my ability to really love myself. What did loving myself really mean to me? I was facing my greatest challenge, which was to love myself unconditionally just as God does, and to stay with that Love for myself and for life itself and to stay out of issues. Loving myself not because of my achievements, my service to others, my work, how I looked, what others thought of me but more because I am a truly precious expression of life itself. I had tapped into this knowing, understanding and experience many times throughout my lifetime and

147

somehow I allowed it to get covered over again. In love and out of love over and over again with myself and others. What I came to realise was that I was never 'out' of love I was just covered over or caught up with the issues. In a sense 'not seeing the wood for the tree's '. Somehow I had learned to be the perfectionist, constantly on the go, without stopping to listen to my deeper self, not being conscious of conflicts that I was having within myself. I ended up exhausting myself trying to pack in all that I thought I was supposed to be doing and should be doing, trying to fix all around me, instead of heeding the many prompts from my own deeper self. Many issues presented and as a result many difficulties. My attention went on to the issues and away from living life itself leaving me so deeply unhappy and my body as a result was shutting down. My dearest friend Tony shared this insight with me and it totally resonated with the deepest part of myself. I am forever grateful for the healing and the magic that

Tony gave to me on that magical afternoon in June 2015, as this was a true awakening and turning point for me. In that truly special time with Tony, I felt he truly saw me as he always did with such love and no judgement, how I really was within myself and within my life, what I dearly valued and how I was to reconnect to my life again.

Being diagnosed with cancer to me was a 'gift' in that it totally stopped me in my tracks. It stopped me continuing down the path I was on, which was getting into issues, not just my own but especially taking on my families and others issues. I realised I was having issues with their issues instead of having a real relationship with them and a real relationship with myself. Eventually the issues made their way into my tissues.

It gave me the time and space to reflect, to fully reconnect, to listen and fully heed the prompts and direction that comes from the very essence of me which is pure love... It got me to STOP, to LOOK, and to LISTEN - and most importantly to HEED and FOLLOW the direction my own deeper self had for me, which I understand now more than ever, is one of real love for life its self, for myself and for others. In a way it's like awakening in a deeper way to the true meaning of putting my LIFE first, of taking responsibility for myself and honouring my life, having respect for others and for where they are on their journey without judgement. I understand in a deeper way and with a deeper acceptance that we are all on our own personal life journey. I realise how important it is not to loose sight of that understanding and to respect where others are in their own lives without judgement.

Loving the very life that I am, and that I am here to express it in my own unique wonderful way lifts and nourishes my spirit. I am no longer dis-spirited.

I'm hearing that fabulous song in my mind from the Beatles " ALL YOU NEED IS LOVE" as I come to the end of this chapter. What I have learnt through writing and reflecting is that I am an active co-creator of my own life story, creating all the good and fantastic stories and also coping with challenges and managing trauma's. To love, honour and respect myself and others. Transforming a trauma or challenging experience into a coherent story has made the whole experience manageable and truly educational and invaluable to me. I see and feel a wonderful debt within me that is continually evolving, allowing me to grow into being the person I've always wanted to be. It has empowered me to feel and to know that not only can I cope but I can also transform life's traumas into real life learning opportunity's giving me a richer moment-to-moment life experience.

Going forward - what is the greatest gift I can give myself? To love ALL that I AM....

I read a wonderful quote from Wayne W. Dyer; "with everything that has happened to you, you can either feel sorry for yourself or treat what has happened as a gift. Everything is either an opportunity to grow or an obstacle to keep you from growing. You get to choose."

I choose Life, to grow and to give myself complete permission to heal and to explore even more the power of me, my birthright! ….

… And so my next chapter begins…

Chapter 6

Are We Home Yet?

By: Isobelle Burns

We had always lived alone, just the two of us, and that suited us perfectly. No matter where we were, as long as we were together we were as happy as pigs in mud. We ate together, slept together, and played together. We were together in our dreams and in reality- experiencing life together as best friends do. We were inseparable! No one could come between us, and no one could break the bond we had- the bond of a Mother and Daughter.

As a baby, she was very sick and needed twenty-four hour care. She was born with a small four-millimetre hole in her heart- something I had not been informed till her six-week check-up. Imagine my shock to find out they had known all along and thought I did too.

Not long after she was born, she was whisked out of my arms and straight to intensive care in the arms of a nurse, running at top speed. With no explanation, I was left there for the longest five minutes of my life. When I finally managed to see her, she was in a room with just one other baby and dressed - to my dismay – in blue. Propped up at an angle and hooked up to monitors, she seemed to be doing just fine. She had suffered a "blue episode". More than twelve hours passed before I could take her back to my own room. Twelve hours of no sleep, fearing my very touch would shatter her like a delicate glass web. Each time I would visit her I would change her out of her blue clothes and put her back into pink – only to find she was put back into blue clothes again. Doctors would come in to give supportive comments and assure us we were doing a great job. Nurse after nurse would

155

comment - "He's gorgeous" to which I would answer, "yes SHE is!" but the penny never dropped.

Back in my room I finally had the chance to begin my life as a new mother. In between blue episode after blue episode- running back and forth between my room and the nurse's station we started to get to know one another. How very small she was- yet very tall, she had already outgrown newborn booties but wore tiny baby clothes. I adopted the nurses decision not let her lie flat and therefore began to relax – a little. I slept with one eye open with her in my arms and hovering over her during the day.

For the next eight months, I spent every night sleeping in an upright position with her sleeping on her tummy - on mine. The same way you would cradle your newborn, one leg and arm either side. With the addition of pillows either side to prop my arms up and minimise any sliding. Finally we could both enjoy a full night's sleep. This is what gave me the extra determination to protect her from everything thrown at us! I wasn't going to give up that easy.

Unfortunately, three months before her second birthday, we became homeless. I had to make a decision – a very hard one indeed and now as our home was no longer safe for us, that meant a women's refuge for the next few months.

We were forced to leave our large three-bedroom house, full with large rooms, hallways and big gardens. The very home we had started to make a life in-painted walls, first steps, potty training, first birthday, first accident and unforgettable memories.

Our home still wasn't decorated or pretty, fancy or boasting many furnishings but it was our home. It was our safe haven- our sanctuary. This was the only place on the earth we could escape to from the craziness of everyday life. When all you need is a breather from the many people you see every day, from their problems and never ending judgement.

Rathmines

Upon reaching the refuge, I was left in the hands of a member of staff, who I thought would have some compassion and understanding and realize just how tired I was, given the fact that I looked like death and was barely able to stand. Oblivious to the late hour she decided to execute her own detailed interview on the night's events. When would my torture end? Would it ever end? Was I being treated like a victim or a criminal? It was soon pretty clear.

A night's sleep was what I was supposed to have before making my way to the other side of Dublin to collect my daughter. I chose the bottom bunk at the far wall facing the door and tried to sleep. Unfortunately due to non-visible injuries to my rib cage, I couldn't lie down, on my back, side or front, eventually I slept partially propped up with pillows, no medication, and without my daughter. The ice-cold sheets and hospital-like blankets reminded me that I was not at home. The echo of other residents calling to their children in their rooms reached my ears no matter how low they were, made me feel more isolated than ever. The large cement block walls painted a dull creamy yellow in shiny prison-like paint with dark grey open wardrobes. To have to sleep in a strange place, in a strange bed, with strange people was nothing compared to the absence of my daughters warmth in my arms. She was my safety blanket and my peace.

With my daughter back with me the next day and little or no belongings with us, we tried to make the most of our day, trying to understand our surroundings and the people we were now forced to share them with. We were given a squashed room with two sets of bunk beds and a single bed. Our first day went by in a blur- yet brought back to earth when the sound of the church bell and any knock on the door would send her into a panic, running for cover. This shocked me to the core. Why was she doing this? Had she seen anything? Had she heard? She was three months shy of two yet she was acting beyond her years. I was worried.

The next few days passed with trips to the doctor for painkillers to numb my rib cage and to check my neck as I'd lost my voice- as a result from the hand around my neck.

We were introduced to everyone as though we were new students to a class. I had no interest in meeting anyone or getting to know any of the women sharing the refuge, but for my daughters sake I went along. She didn't deserve everything that had happened and her new circumstances. She needed the normality of friends and playtime, of having a routine similar to her old one and to be sheltered from anything that harmed her. This proved impossible there so ten weeks later I was forced to make yet another hard decision- it was time to go into homeless accommodation- Sunnybank!

Capuchin

I'd like to say our lives came to a complete stop when we became homeless, and on so many levels it did. Yet there were silver linings that came around just in the nick of time to pick us up a little higher from our knees. There were not enough of these to keep our sanity but we appreciated them all the same. It became quite clear to keep a firm hold while we still could recognize them. One of these was "Lukes" or as it is formally called -Capuchin!

Whilst many other people were making their way to work, we were on our way to the homeless centre. This had become a big part of our everyday lives and in

many ways our only glimpse of normality. Amira
could eat safely, see friendly faces and play happily.
Capuchin was a place for many people from all over
Dublin to come and eat, wash and avail of the doctor.
In our case –food, company and a book for comfort.
On a daily basis hundreds of people came to this
centre. It was always full to the brim so not many
stayed more than a half hour. Rows of tables lined the
walls and floor with the addition of a cornered off and
protected area. This area was the family area. All
children were to eat here, to be kept away from the
reality of the habits of the other side. Many people
would come to the divide between the sides when
collecting their cutlery and selflessly hand over their
only desert (sometimes just a banana or donut) to the
children. Three long tables squished inside and two
baby chairs available meant rotation was necessary on
busy days. If you were finished eating you would have
to leave to let others in. This wasn't particularly

welcomed when the weather poured. We would be left to traipse the streets under the cover of raincoats and black bags until dinnertime, when we would return.

Where is Clonskeagh?

Finding our new shelter wasn't as easy as we would have expected. An address on a piece of paper simply wasn't enough to follow in an area unknown to us. What a joke it seemed. A single mother with a young child of two years to traipse to the far side of Dublin with no idea of where, or how far to go. Not a single person seemed to know the address or want to give directions.

With roads lined with scrambled numbers I realised this was going to be a very long evening. It was already becoming late and this meant I could be in trouble- and on day one! With such tight rules applied to each tenant, being late was not an option. Being late meant lock out and possibly cancellation of your stay. Without explanation or apology- as of course what could your reason for staying out at night be? This was a nightmare we did not need.

Clonskeagh seemed to be a quiet, lonely place as we retraced our steps yet again along the row of darkened houses. Slowly peering in to catch a glimpse of any sign that we were in the right place. House after house was accompanied with bitter disappointment. Cold, tired and hungry, I gave up many times. The only comfort was the crunch of the heavy gravel under my feet to fill the silence. Passing each pillar became more confusing as time went on. It seemed as though there was a pattern – yet one I couldn't follow or understand. Each house had two pillars, one on either side of its gates. One pillar wrote "5" and the other "10". The next house followed this strange pattern, one pillar "6" and the other "12". This continued up the road- 5-10.....6-

12...7-14. What? The other side of the road did not follow this pattern at all.

We were getting nowhere. The navigation on my phone knew less than me- completely clueless. We finally came across a set of apartments at the bend of the road. "Please let this be it!" I plucked the courage to ring the bell for the number I was given- Nothing! Was there a reception or other number bell I was to ring? This was becoming a joke. This kind of confusion only happened in my nightmares- where nothing made sense- nothing was what it seemed. Was I asleep? I rang again and then gave up. It was already dark now and becoming chilly. Not a single cloud could be seen in the sky-not even the sky could be seen. The glow from the street lamps along the narrow street seemed to dominate all colour.

I spotted a pub/cafe nearby and decided to ask once again for directions. I stood out a mile from the punters partying within. Women splashed with perfume, pearls, and pretty dresses with perfectly styled hair to match. Holding tiny glasses and laughing their hearts out as they relaxed after a week's work. The men in neatly pressed suit shirts and pants with polished shoes, and waxed hair. A few turned as I entered and looked me up and down- assessing my attire. No- I didn't belong. I quickly slipped up to the barman and asked for directions. After he called his work colleague who also couldn't help I slipped back out? Not a single person heard of this address. I was beginning to think it didn't exist.

Heading back down the road again I spotted and arched door- with no bell. Not it. I finally came across what I prayed to be the house I was looking for. Well two. The address I was given gave me two numbers with a dash in-between - 11-14. This did not help, as there were two doors and two gates and a long high fence in between. Which one do I knock? No more than five cars passed by in our time finding our new place. That really brought it home that we were alone. I decided on the house on the right and rang. Nothing. Not again. This was becoming ridiculous. Just as I was giving up, a woman popped her head out from her window and started screaming. Regardless of the quiet street I still couldn't understand a word until I heard a few chosen profanities. "Lovely" I thought. "Please say I'm at the wrong place".

Just as I was about to leave, a short, quiet man appeared at the door and after I explained what I was doing there he assured me I was finally at the right place. With my bags and buggy it was clear to him straight away who I was. He led me through a small hallway with two sets of doors and explained the rules and how things were run then supplied us with keys.

Finally! We were at our next halfway house.

Were Invisible

Many times throughout our lives we witness events that shock us. Whether good or bad, we witness scenes of happiness, disturbance and hatred against loved ones and others. At some point we insist on our own interference with the hunger to put things right but never convert these words and intentions into actions.

Instead of extending a helping hand, we point our fingers and label and oppress them. Yes oppress- something you don't regularly think, it just doesn't occur to us. We are capable and are guilty of being such oppressors. We can never comprehend- that is, until we experience it first-hand. Unless we become helpless in a turn of events that leave us at the end of others arms, as the ones being judged.   Would we learn from it? Would we retain anything from this experience over our lifetime? Or shed it at the first sight of normality in our lives. Are our brains capable of overcoming such an imperfect disability to adapt to knowledge without the accompanying of sparkles, dazzling lights and promises?

It seems as though we have become ignorant of our senses. Our instinct to survive has developed in the wrong direction. Have we skipped steps or become partially blind on the way to adulthood? Can we blame our society- as we often do?

We have lost our sight- the ability to recognise a lesson to learn from, a person in need, a sign to follow, a warning of danger...

We have lost our hearing- the ability to listen to what's right and disregard what's wrong, to listen to good advice, to help distinguish between good and bad, to answer to someone's plight, call for help...

We have lost our voice- the ability to speak up when the need is clearly present, for those who cannot speak for themselves, the ability to give the right advice, to be honest and speak the truth...

Writers Biographies:

Salwa Elhamamsy

Salwa Mohamed Elhamamsy is an Egyptian writer who writes short stories, travel literature and opinion articles in national newspapers. She belongs to the nineties generations of Egyptian writers, she is interested in humanitarian social issues. She is also trying to revive the old heritage of Egyptian contemporary writing in a new and socially reformist way. She has been writing short stories and editorials since the late eighties.

https://www.amazon.com/Salwa-Elhamamsy/e/B00XUSHBKG

http://www.arabwomenwriters.com/index.php/2014-05-03-16-02-58/2014-05-03-19-10-32/salwa-elhamamsy

Patricia Steele

Patricia says, I'm a west coast girl that moved to the east coast and back again. Twice. My imagination has always been etched in music, color and rose-colored glasses. I've had crazy characters and stories banging and fluttering around in my head, dying to get out, since I was old enough to hold a pen. I'm a fan of historical fiction filled with adventure and romance. And I'm addicted to genealogy! My sense of humor runs a little rampant at times, I'm no stranger to laughter, and I love a good anticipation scene. I am proud to state that The Girl Immigrant, the first novel in my Spanish Pearls Series, is being whisked off my shelves. The second book in the series, Silván Leaves, is now available. My next project is a memoir titled, Fairy Dust to Daffodils about my daughter and her fight with Cystic Fibrosis.

Michael Whelan

A carpenter by profession, Michael continues to fulfil a
lifelong passion for travel and adventure. 'Borderline'
is a snapshot from his most recent exploit; a solo cycle
along the Silk Road from Pakistan to China. He lives
with his wife and daughter in County Waterford,
Ireland.

Aisling Meath

Aisling Meath is a freelance broadcast journalist based in West Cork Ireland. She has worked as a researcher for RTE, TG4 and in French TV production. She is a contributor to the Southern Star and Irish Examiner newspapers.

Madeline Page

Madeline Page is a wellness coach and has only recently started to write. She is very passionate about life and especially helping people to reach their highest potential so they can experience true health and real happiness.

She has worked as a yoga and health instructor for almost thirty years and is currently recovering from Non Hodgkin lymphoma Cancer.

Her recent experience with Cancer has inspired her to write for a memoir chapter in the hope that her own experience may shine light to others.

Madeline lives in Dublin, Ireland.

Marley Isobelle Burns

She is an Irish based writer and artist living in Dublin. She enjoys writing about realistic life experiences and also those that live only in ones imagination. Writing broadens the mind to experience the detail in life that might go undiscovered.

Index:

----------------------------END

Made in the USA
Charleston, SC
14 January 2017